THE PRESIDENT'S SMILE

WASHINGTON CLOSE-UPS

INTIMATE VIEWS OF
SOME PUBLIC FIGURES

BY

EDWARD G. LOWRY

259.

WITH ILLUSTRATIONS

BOSTON AND NEW YORK
HOUGHTON MIFFLIN COMPANY
The Riverside Press Cambridge
1921

TO
S. E. L.
AND
E. L. L.

NOTE

Some of the chapters in this book have appeared, in part, in substance, or in whole, in *The New Republic*, *Collier's Weekly*, and *The Weekly Review*. Grateful acknowledgment is made to the editors of these journals for permission to reprint here such of the material as has been published in their columns.

E. G. L.

Seven Gates Farm
    Martha's Vineyard

CONTENTS

ILLUSTRATIONS

WASHINGTON CLOSE-UPS

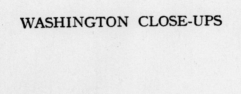

WASHINGTON CLOSE-UPS

259

THE WASHINGTON SCENE

ÆONS upon æons agone, when the bat-winged ptero-dactyl swooped down relentlessly upon its prey, — I mean to say a long time ago, — this humid cup in the hills that is now the Washington scene may have been different; it must have been. With that we have no present concern.

But Washington itself; the Washington of the organic act, of the Adamses, John and Quincy, of Martin Van Buren, Millard Fillmore, Rutherford B. Hayes, Benjamin Harrison, William H. Taft, and Woodrow Wilson, is the Washington of Warren G. Harding. Regard the eternal changelessness of the two stone legs of King Ozymandias in the desert of Egypt and attune your mind to the tale I have to tell.

Come with me into Mr. Harding's front yard and let us sit under a flowering magnolia and leisurely, as becomes the pure in heart and detached in mind, talk about the familiar apparitions who inhabit these pleasant walks and tinker with our destiny.

It passes belief how little is known about Washington by the country at large, and yet no city is more written about. Still, it is hardly ever justly appraised by the people at home. They seem to see it through a refracting and magnifying haze. New York and Chicago and San Francisco and St. Louis and New Orleans they know and can justly estimate. They are visualized clearly, but it is curiously true that almost every newcomer to Washington and every visitor suffers a sort of stage fright.

O. Henry in one of his stories tells about a cowboy going to New York and being diffident before New Yorkers, until he discovered they were people "just like Grover Cleveland and Geronimo and the Watson boys." No citizen of Danville, Illinois, or Pike County, Missouri, or Springfield, Massachusetts, would make any average American tongue-tied or step on his feet with embarrassment. Yet those three places have furnished the last three Speakers of the House of Representatives, and the Speaker of the House is a great personage in Washington. Tourists to the Capitol peer into his room with awe, and nudge one another furtively and say "That's him," when they pass him by happy chance in a corridor. Then they go home and talk about it for days and days.

I do not know why it is that individually the Senators and Representatives and Cabinet members are always so awe-inspiring to their fellow countrymen, while collectively it has always been the fashion to disparage them. The late Henry Adams was the very greatest of Washington correspondents, though I should have been afraid so to describe him in his presence. He spent a lifetime, from Lincoln's administration through Roosevelt's, looking at the Washington scene with clear eyes and interpreting the marionettes with the coolest, most detached mind that has ever been brought to that occupation. When I used to talk with him in the latter years of his life I found to my dismay that all of my slowly acquired discoveries he had known since the sixties, and some of them were known to his grandfather before him. Some of his impressions gathered between 1840 and 1869 might have been written to-day looking at the present assemblage here.

It is as true now as it was in President Taylor's administration that Senators are a distinct species, and that continuous service in Congress produces — a Congressman. They have their own easily discernible vocational stigmata. They are a distinct sort of human being and as easily distinguishable, once you know them, as a raw oyster from a cup of tea. The type reproduces with astonishing fidelity, despite the greatest moral, social, and political convulsions.

Our system is so arranged that Congressmen must necessarily spend two thirds of their time making arrangements to endeavor to ensure their reëlection. I do not make any outcry against the system, but it is a thing to be pointed out. Six thousand night telegrams properly distributed will agitate Congress like a strong wind blowing over wheat, so sensitive is it to the possible political effect of anything it may do or leave undone.

I remember that President Wilson, who never got on with Washington easily, never fitted into the scene, and, to me, always seemed rather afraid of its allure and subtle charm, once said: "The city of Washington is in some respects self-contained, and it is easy there to forget what the rest of the United States is thinking about. I count it a fortunate circumstance that almost all the windows of the White House and its offices open upon unoccupied spaces that stretch to the banks of the Potomac and then out into Virginia and on to the heavens themselves, and that as I sit there I can constantly forget Washington and remember the United States. Not that I would intimate that all of the United States lies south of Washington, but there is a serious thing back of my thought. If you think too much about being reëlected, it is very difficult to be worth reëlecting. You are so apt to forget that the comparatively small number of persons, numerous as they seem to be when they swarm, who come to Washington to ask for things, do not constitute an important proportion of the population of the country, that it is constantly necessary to come away from Washington and renew one's contacts with the people who do not swarm there, who do not ask for anything, but who do trust you without their personal counsel to do your duty. Unless a man gets these contacts he grows weaker and weaker. He needs them as Hercules needed the touch of mother earth. If you lifted him up too high or he lifts himself too high, he loses the contact and therefore loses the inspiration."

Washington cries aloud to be written about in an intimate, amusing way. It is somehow different from other social settlements on the broad expanse of our continent. The town has a distinctive social life of its own with a flavor and quality slightly tinctured with the modes and manners of "abroad." It has, too, a seductive charm and glamour all its own. The oddity and part of the charm of the Washington condition is just this, that while it has the social framework of a world capital the chief official personages who people the scene are villagers with a villager's outlook and a villager's background. This makes for unexpected ellipses and provides conversation. Henry James called Washington the "City of Conversation": "Washington talks about herself, and about almost nothing else: falling superficially, indeed, on that ground, but into line with the other Capitals. . . . It is in positive quest of an identity of some sort, much rather — an identity other than merely functional and technical — that Washington goes forth, encumbered with no ideal of avoidance or escape: it is about herself *as* the City of Conversation precisely that she incessantly converses; adorning the topic, moreover, with endless ingenuity and humor. But that, absolutely, remains the case; which thus becomes one of the most thorough, even if probably one of the most natural and of the happiest, cases of collective self-consciousness that one knows."

I couldn't refrain from quoting that bit of rich and experienced condensation and observation because it is precisely the whole story. People take such dreadful risks when they venture to approach or touch a subject that a master has laid a benevolent and passing hand upon, even if ever so lightly and in passing. Henry James stopped with Henry Adams when he was last in Washington. These two are the only men who have ever written about this national capital with a sureness and skill that illumined and interpreted their subject. Many others have been conscious, but, as it proved, vaguely and dimly, of the scene they have sought to portray.

It all comes down to this: Washington is a curious and delightful place; it is so full of the most refreshing and striking contrasts. The capital of a country of a hundred million, and the center of statesmanship, diplomacy, and high politics, its citizens write hot and hasty letters to the powers that be, protesting that hawks devour their Pekin ducks, and that rabbits come after their corn. They argue gravely the constitutionality of their right of defense against these depredations.

Washington is the most feminine of all cities. It has grace and loveliness and many wanton wiles, and, above all, that elusive quality and attribute that for want of a better name we call charm. Its seductiveness and glamour have drawn many a good, homespun citizen away from the hay, grain, and feed business, where he belonged, into the political morass of office-holders. It has the same effect on small-town people that Cleopatra had on Anthony; it makes them forget their homefolks and have dreams which do not come true.

Politicians are great men in Washington and get their names in the newspapers, and hold their jobs just so long as they remember their home towns. When they forget their origins; when they begin to think of themselves as being "big men" in and of themselves rather than as delegated spokesmen for their constituencies, they wither and die. I often think of Washington as being like a flower show. Nothing grows here, but every community sends what it deems at the moment to be its choicest product. So long as these budding, flowering plants remember that their tap-root is in Augusta, Maine; or Terre Haute; or Red Oak, Iowa; or Tuscaloosa, Alabama, and must be watered and nourished there, they thrive; but when they forget it, they become just cut flowers and their end is at hand.

So in this scene life proceeds from one crisis to another. But do not despair of the Republic. The only thing one can be sure about in a crisis or situation or condition at Washington is that it is not un-precedented; it has happened before. Washington can-not be seen intelligently or to any effect without a background. It produces crises and periods of welter

and confusion in such regularly recurring cycles as to
be almost susceptible to the formulation of a law of
natural phenomena. Certainly the sons and descend-
ants of Jeremiah have rended their garments, beat
their breasts, and made loud lamentation before the
Capitol and the White House after each of our war
periods. They sat about in bewilderment as they sit
now, and will again, saying to one another, "Was
there ever such an extraordinary situation? Was there
ever such another mess as we find ourselves in now?
Was there ever such another set of dolts, knaves, and
incompetents in command of our destinies?" The
answer is: There was. This is not the first time that
the wind has moaned through the rigging.

What Washington is at any period it has been and
fearfully will be again. It stumbles, but it never falls.
Against this background and in this scene, I ask, by
your leave, to exhibit some of the apparitions and
figures I have encountered. They are a diverse lot and
all of them have interested me, as I hope they will
interest you.

HARDING: THE GREAT EMOLLIENT

POLITICALLY Mr. Harding belongs to the same age, era, epoch, or period as the wooden Indians who used to stand so massively, so passively, and so innocuously in front of cigar shops. He is as old-fashioned as that. A flower of the period before safety razors, when all the barber shops had shelves for their customers' gilt-lettered private shaving-mugs, and the *Police Gazette* passed from hand to hand on Sunday mornings while the hay, grain, and feed man and the elderly harness-maker took a fearful joy in gazing at Pauline Hall's delectable and columnar legs. Then to church before a fried-chicken dinner, a nap, and a walk with the children in the afternoon.

Pastoral days, peaceful days, idyllic days, but, now, alas! gone where the woodbine twineth, as the poet said. No flivvers; no collective bargaining; no high cost of living; no small and oppressed nationalities; the railroad problem was how to get a pass; no "industrial unrest"; no Reds; no grisly specters of Soviets; no coal shortage; no mandates or Article X; hired men worked all day every day, and on Sundays put on a hat with a red lining specially designed for the country trade and went buggy-riding; no mass urgings and surgings toward God knows what goal.

Such were the palmy days in which were formed the

character, habits, and political philosophy of Warren Gamaliel Harding. He has not changed with the times.

The President can "keynote." I have heard him. "Keynoting" implies the ability to make melodic noises and give the impression of passionately and torrentially moving onward and upward while warily standing still. Temperament under perfect control does the trick. It has its attendant dangers sometimes. Once upon a time there was a young fellow tried it with a girl down in Georgia. She was a nice, sensible, common-sense sort of girl, and she liked the boy. He used to come over to her house nearly every night and they would sit on the porch behind the honeysuckle and morning-glory vines. The boy could talk, and nearly every night he would play her a piece on his bazoo. She liked it, too; but, when she would go upstairs to bed and, while she was combing her hair, add up what he had said, she couldn't remember anything that would warrant her in beginning to pick out her bridesmaids. Nothing was happening and time was getting along. One night, under the influence of a soft moon and a mocking-bird, the boy began to silver tongue. She stood it just as long as she could, and then she called for a showdown. She put her hand on his arm. "Claude," she said softly, "if that's a proposal, I'm your huckleberry; but if it's a description of the scenery, look out for the dog."

I think Mr. Harding ought to know that story; that's why I tell it. The present temper and mood of

THE PRESIDENT AT WORK AND AT PLAY

most folks these days seems to be to get down to cases and find out what ails us.

It was privily urged upon one of the functionaries of Mr. Wilson's *entourage* a little while before that administration came to an end that it would be a shrewd and clever thing to do, a good "publicity stunt," to throw open the gates of the White House and make the grounds and the accessible state rooms of the presidential edifice free again to the public. The suggestion was denied admittance. Had it been heeded, Mr. Harding would have been deprived of what proved to be a most effective gesture as he began his term of residence at Number 1600 Pennsylvania Avenue.

It beats all what a change has come over the spirit and manners and disposition of this town since Mr. Harding came in. I don't know how long it will last. It is too idyllic to last forever. Partly this new manifestation of peace on earth good-will to men is due to opening the White House gates, but mostly it is due to Mr. Harding himself. He has undeniably made a good start. He made an immensely favorable first impression. He got started off on the right foot. He quickly won for himself a great body of local favorable public opinion. That was so startling and vivid a contrast to the condition that had prevailed here for some time that it assumed, temporarily at least, an appearance of tremendous significance and importance.

In the local area now under observation, at any

rate, the normalcy, so long ago set forth as one of the chief ends to be attained, has been achieved.

For a long time the social-political atmosphere of Washington had been one of bleak and chill austerity suffused and envenomed by hatred of a sick chief magistrate that seemed to poison and blight every ordinary human relationship and finally brought to a virtual stoppage every routine function of the Government. It was a general condition of stagnation and aridity that had come to affect everybody here. The White House was isolated. It had no relation with the Capitol or the local resident and official community. Its great iron gates were closed and chained and locked. Policemen guarded its approaches. It was in a void apart. Almost from the beginning it had seemed to the sensitive local intelligence to exhale a chill and icy disdain for the chief subordinate figures and personages who under the President comprise the personnel of the Washington community. This may have been imagination, but it had the full effect of a reality. It all made for bleakness and bitterness and a general sense of frustration and unhappiness.

Now the chief thing to report at this early period of the new dispensation is that this miasmatic vapor has been dissipated overnight. The Washington atmosphere to-day is that of Old Home Week or a college class reunion. The change is amazing. The populace is on a broad grin — old familiar figures have reappeared out of an eight-year seclusion. Countenances that one feared had lost the art or knack of beaming now radiate warmth and light and good cheer. Distinctly the sunny side is up. Indeed, I venture to suspect that not since the halcyon days when Sandford and Merton sat in the garden with the ineffable Mr. Barlow, and discoursed together on the joys and rewards of a virtuous life, has there been so much of sweetness and harmony and light susceptible to local observation and sympathetic record. It is just sweet, as Grizel used to put it to Tommy the while her eyes were little wells of gladness.

It must have been like this aforetime when the morning stars sang together and the little hills skipped for joy. For there is no remembrance with us of former days.

It is now possible for any decent citizen of the Republic, becomingly appareled, to enter the east portico or extension of the White House and proceed along the corridor or passage, where were displayed the fish-plates, sauce-boats, and other ceramic remains of the Millard Fillmore and Franklin Pierce administrations, and so on up the broad stairs that lead to the historic East Room, where once the White House washing hung and which more recently has been given over to private moving-picture shows for the diversion of an ill President. From here it is but a step to ascend or descend the chromatic scale of the presidential parlors — Red, Blue, Green. This historic little journey over ground long an inviolate sanctuary has been taken by thousands since the inaugural.

In the very first flush of the new freedom, eager, ardent visitors stood in a compact mass under the north portico or main entrance and stared their fill at all who came and went from the White House. Some of the bolder ventured up the steps and did a collective Little-Mabel-with-her-face-against-the-pane through the front windows. I do not cite this as a model of good manners or as a practice that should be encouraged, but it gave thousands pleasure, it satisfied an eager curiosity and craving for an actual contact with and sight of the occupants of the White House, and it proved to be as tactful and effective a gesture as could have been devised to indicate that a page had been turned in our political history.

The news has gone all over the country that the White House is open again, and it has been given an interpretation and significance far beyond its value. I report it here as one of the things that helped Mr. Harding most in the opening days of his administration and gave him a decided impetus along the highway of public favor. It has given him a stock of good opinion which he will have need to draw upon, unless I miss my guess.

But it is in the White House offices, where Mr. Harding spends his days, that the questing analyst finds in greatest profusion and richness the signs and indications of the new order. These rooms and carpeted passages, lately so deserted and forlorn, are now packed and running over. All of the people you used to read about in the newspapers twelve years ago, when Mr. Taft became President, are there; and a lot of new ones that you never heard of, but will if they have any luck. Just at the moment these patriots and fellow countrymen, now rescued from their long hibernation, want jobs or have friends who want jobs. Some few of them, however, just want to "pay their respects," revisit an old familiar scene and perhaps meet a kindly correspondent who will put a little piece in the papers about them. It is these recurring figures, long absent from this environment and now so unaffectedly glad to be back and on terms with the White House, who give the atmosphere of Old Home Week to these pleasant walks and meetings.

My first contact with Mr. Harding himself was as fleeting and casual as the kiss of two billiard balls, and yet I brought away with me three bright and vivid, if vagrant and irrelevant, impressions. The first is that like all Ohio statesmen he wears trousers that are too long. I don't know why this should be so, but it is. I think the feeling against "high-water pants" as indicating a countryman or "hick" must have been peculiarly virulent in Ohio thirty or forty years ago, for all her present generation of public men like their trousers to hang in folds about their ankles.

This, at any rate, was the explanation given me by one of the State's Congressmen years ago when we discussed this esoteric topic. I hadn't thought of this for a long time until I noticed that Mr. Harding rigidly conforms to the convention. Subsequent contacts developed that some one had been at him and shortened his suspenders. It makes all the difference.

The second impression I brought away is that the President has, at least, two pet words that he uses constantly. They are "becoming" and "seemly." I think it will be observed of him, as he becomes a more intimate and accustomed apparition to all of us, that he cannot talk very long on any subject without using one of these two words and, perhaps, both of them. I present this facet to the Freudians. Let them make what they can of it.

The third impression that I have to set down was the first and the strongest Mr. Harding makes upon every one. I mean the essential kindliness and kindness that fairly radiate from him. He positively gives out even to the least sensitive a sense of brotherhood and innate good-will toward his fellow man. With it he imparts a certain sense of simpleness and trustfulness, an easy friendliness, an acceptance of people he meets as good fellows. It is in his eyes, in his voice, in his manners. I'll wager that saying "no" is one of the most difficult things he does. Abou Ben Adhem, I believe, would have taken to him like a shot.

This outstanding trait of easy good-fellowship and good-will was exhibited to unusual advantage in his first meeting with the Washington correspondents. It had been arranged for Mr. Harding to receive the writing men at twelve-thirty o'clock on the day of the first cabinet meeting, and after that session had ended, but it was one-thirty before the correspondents were invited into the circular presidential office. At that time Mr. Harding made himself easier of access than any good dentist, for, at least, with a dentist in fair practice one has to make an appointment a week in advance, but, in the beginning, the President allowed some Senators and such-like important persons to "run in" on him. This easy, friendly practice, which Mr. Taft also had in his first days, threw his whole schedule of appointments out of gear, and caused him to run behind the time-table the competent White House staff arranged for him. Mr. Harding will have to guard his time, as he will soon learn. He is the most besought person, perhaps, in the whole world, and his hours must be carefully apportioned among the be-siegers lest he be overwhelmed.

By a happy chance I also attended Mr. Wilson's first meeting with the Washington correspondents, and, as there can be no fair trial of speed without a pace maker, I remembered that chill and correct per-formance, for the chief interest in Washington these days is in the sharp and striking contrast between what is and what was. Mr. Wilson stood behind his desk, his visitors filed in and stood in a thickened crescent before him. There was a pause, a cool silence, and presently some one ventured a tentative question. It was answered crisply, politely, and in the fewest possible words. A pleasant time was not had by all.

Mr. Harding showed another approach. He met the incoming throng at the door and shook hands with every one of them. For most of them he had an individual word of greeting. Apparently it was the most natural thing in the world for him to do. He made it a very simple, unaffected action. The men had come in such numbers that they completely encircled the room in a triple ring. Mr. Harding was in the center of the circle, very much at his ease, leaning against and half sitting upon the edge of his flat-topped desk. He did not wait for questions, but began to talk, an easy, gossipy chat about the first cabinet meeting of his administration. He went on to other things. He knew the professional interests of his hearers. He told them "the story" of what they came to hear. He talked frankly, but not indiscreetly. The whole arranged, premeditated contact was free of constraint or any hint of stiffness.

Day by day Mr. Harding is being bodied forth to the country as a genial, kindly, generous, good-hearted, big fellow who loves his fellow man, who loves simple things, who is without austerity or bitterness, who is not cantankerous, who is easy to get along with. In point of fact this all may be true. The impression is given out partly naturally and involuntarily by Mr. Harding himself in his daily relations with his visitors and partly by skilled and unostentatious arrangement.

Almost every day delegations come to see the President. Almost every one of them is taken out on the stretch of turf between the south portico and the executive offices, and in front of the latticed enclosures where the White House laundry is hung, and photographed with Mr. Harding. Almost all of these photographs are reproduced in the newspapers. You must have seen many of them. They show Mr. Harding with a kindly smile on his face. He takes a good picture, and his bold features reproduce well in the coarse-screen half-tones that the newspapers use. It is effective publicity and quite legitimate. These reproduced scenes of the chief magistrate among his people gratify a natural craving. The people who are taken with the President and their friends like the pictures. The newspapers print them because they are news and because they interest readers. In this way you may have seen Mr. Harding in the White House garden with printers, golf players, Boy Scouts, Girl Scouts, boys who wanted a subscription for a swimming-pool, Einstein of relativity fame with his hair every which way — as Senator Spooner's used to stand — and looking as startled as a Thomson's gazelle; in brief, representatives of every type and group of men and women this broad Republic can offer.

I do not think Mr. Harding has greatly altered the opinion that was held before of his substance, his qualities, and his capacities, but by his kindliness and affability he has notably affected and increased leniency of judgment. I have noticed that people who come in contact with him cease to speak of him or judge him detachedly. They say good-humoredly when his name comes up, "But after all he is a good scout. He wants to do what is right. Give him a chance. He's got a hard job to fill and he is doing his best."

That feeling is a decided and enviable asset for any President to have. It extends to the press. The correspondents still attend in unprecedented numbers Mr. Harding's bi-weekly audiences. They find these meetings useful. They get news. These contacts are reproduced in a thousand places. The President is presented as he presents himself with all his native kindliness and appealing qualities to the fore.

So far then has Mr. Harding disclosed himself to the resident microscopists, as he stands in the porch of his high adventure and great emprise. The quality he has shown the correspondents has had its effect upon the Senate and all of Washington. He has revealed himself as the great emollient that was needed to soothe, to heal, and to relax the angry, inflamed, jangled, querulous local condition and situation. But this is only the beginning. Whether he has sterner qualities, whether he has toughness of fiber, whether he can endure strains and stresses, whether he can withstand pressure, whether he has taste and discrimination — in fine, whether he is a strong man fit to be President, must yet be proved.

COOLIDGE: FOSTER-CHILD OF SILENCE

THE elections of 1920 imported into the City of Conversation, as one of its necessary consequences, perhaps the oddest and most singular apparition this vocal and articulate settlement has ever known : a politician who does not, who will not, who seemingly cannot talk. A well of silence. A center of stillness.

Moreover, it appears from the meager record that he thinks of himself as Peter Pan, the boy who never grew up to be a man.

We had, of course, all heard of Calvin Coolidge ; that he had been City Councilman, City Solicitor, Court Clerk, State Representative, Mayor, State Senator, Lieutenant-Governor, and Governor in Massachusetts ; that he had held one public job after another virtually continuously since 1899 ; that being in place and in politics was with him a vocation and an avocation. But the man himself as a social human being was not known at all. There was a bright curiosity to be satisfied.

Presiding over the Senate is the least of the duties of the Vice-President of the United States in the Washington scheme of things. What time he spends at the Capitol saying, "Does the Senator from South Dakota yield to the Senator from Mississippi?" or, "The Senator from New Hampshire suggests the absence of a quorum. The clerk will call the roll," or, when the calendar is being called, "The bill will be passed over," is his period of reflection and digestion. His day's work really begins when he gets to his hotel in the evening and finds his dress-clothes laid out on the bed and Mrs. Coolidge tells him, "We are dining with Senator Whosis to-night and you must be dressed and ready to leave here at a quarter to eight." His dress-clothes are his working clothes; the overalls of a Vice-President.

By tradition and precedent the Vice-President has become the official diner-out of the Administration. Every night from November until May he must sally forth in his glad raiment and eat for his party and his chief. He and the potted palms that the close observer of official life notes being hauled from one house to another every afternoon during the season are social fixtures. No big dinner is complete without both of them. The palms stand in the corners and on the stairways.

Anciently it was a game, mildly diverting, to scratch one's name on the under side of the fronds and then keep tab to see how many times one encountered the same palms during the winter season. The palms are background, but the Vice-President is essentially foreground. He sits on the right of the hostess. He is the chief figure of the feast. The palms are, or are supposed to be, decorative. The Vice-President seldom or never is. The theory is that he is witty and amusing, or

GOVERNOR AND MRS. COOLIDGE
A Costume for a Campaign Picture

learned and informative, or a well of deep inside stuff about current political affairs.

Now as it turns out Mr. Coolidge is none of these things. To the whole of Washington, social and political, to this juncture, he presents an impenetrable blank. He dines out with the best of them. Never a night elapses that the big closed car placed at his service by the fond taxpayers does not convey him to a dinner party. No soup, however thick or thin, deters him, no fish, however disguised by the pallid, viscous goo the chefs seem to like, daunts him, and thence south through the entrée to the ice. And all in perfect silence.

> No hammer fell, no ponderous axes rung;
> Like some tall palm the noiseless fabric sprung.
> Majestic silence!

But I must say it is hard on the ladies. They often talk about it. They are supposed to make him have a good time. And having a good time at dinner is popularly supposed to be indicated by a light rattle of small talk. One hears that Mr. Coolidge feels sometimes that he is not doing all that is expected of him, for there are vague current reports that he asks wonderingly, "What do they talk about? I hear them and see them all about me, all at it, but what do they find to say?" One agreeable woman was the nine days' wonder and envy of all Washington because she made him laugh one night at dinner. She never would give the recipe or tell what she said. "I am going to use it again next winter," she declared thriftily.

But every one who has contrived to strike a response from the close-mouthed and eminent figure has not been so reticent. Some of the ladies have told the formula they have used to effect an entrance. From them I learn that the equivalent of open sesame to one small compartment of conversation is an appreciative reference to Vermont. It does not disclose great vistas, nor does it reveal anything that is not already set down in the present-day geographies, but it does serve to provoke a mild simulation of dinner-table chatter. The subject has, moreover, an apparently unending interest. It can be employed four or five times by the same person. And so it comes about that some, at least, women, who are virtually sure to sit beside Mr. Coolidge when they are at dinner together, have made an intensive study of Vermont; its geography, its climate, its mineral and agricultural resources, its population, its scenery, the conformation of its hills and the configuration of its valleys, its industries, its census figures — everything, in fine, but its politics. That is something that is never spoken of. And when you come to think of it, the natural resources of Vermont, such as they are, are quite the safest and sanest subject in the world, as a subject of conversation which may be repeated. They never got anybody into trouble. And that, of course, is something.

I gather that our hero has always been like this; that from his boyhood he has dreaded meeting people if it involved exchanging words with them. It makes

his career as a politician, in so vocal and clamorous a
constituency as ours, all the more conspicuous and
odd. He is never seen in public places. He does not
consort with groups as do other politicians. He is
close, close, close, and as detached as a villa site. His
letters are even briefer than his spoken words. One
that I know about consists merely of one word and the
initials "C. C." If this is a fair sample, and I assume
that it is, when his life and letters come to be published, they can be issued on one octavo postal card.

In common with every one else at Washington I
have been eager to pluck out the heart of Mr. Coolidge's mystery, to discover what sort of man he
is, to establish a basis for appraisal. And all in vain,
for he has revealed nothing, disclosed nothing. He has
been described and observed as intently as was possible
under the circumstances in the crush preceding the
largest and gayest of dinner parties, standing quite
still and saying not a blessed word, though all about
him were babble and laughter and conversation. He
didn't seem ill at ease or embarrassed or tongue-tied.
He was just still. Silent upon a peak in Darien is no
name for it. He gave no appearance of being about to
say something presently. It was an absolute calm.
Old Ironsides at anchor lay in the harbor of Mahon.
The waves to sleep had gone — that sort of thing. Not
a leaf stirring. It was impressive — and he so small.
A big man can be as monosyllabic as he pleases, but
more is expected of slight men.

One sought in vain an account of the experiences of those veterans of forlorn hopes who in the devoted pursuance of social duties had dashed themselves against the ice barrier. They had nothing to tell. Over the Alps lay Italy, they thought, but none of them had won the summit, and so they couldn't be sure that the view was worth the climb.

The only thing left to do was to go back and search the records, to exhume fossil remains, to study the narratives left by the explorers who had been on the same trail. When President Meiklejohn of Amherst, in the course of his duty, conferred the degree of Doctor of Laws on Mr. Coolidge, he complimented him on teaching the value of "adequate brevity." He could not have done less. He might easily have gone on and done more. What may be termed Mr. Coolidge's "short game" with our common tongue is worthy of all the admiring comments that can be bestowed upon it. But his lightness and delicacy of touch in sinking his short putts when he has got the English language on the green approaches the marvelous. He is a master of the reversible short sentence that can be read from either direction without losing the force of its impact.

A paper of his on the nature of politics ends with the sentence, "Destiny is in you." Just like that. "Destiny is in you." It means — whatever you want it to mean. It is compact. It is polished. It is sententious, and it gives all the appearance of being a distillation of profound thought.

One night in the long ago a press agent came to our newspaper to tell the dramatic reporter about a dancer he was bringing to our town and how light-footed she was. He was voluble in his praise of her fairy feet. "Listen," he said; "this little lady could walk on bubbles from the Battery to Harlem Bridge and never bust a bub." And so he whom I now sing walks circumspectly through the lush meadows of English speech, never crushing a flower, while he plucks his modest posies. He diversifies his literary nosegays.

A phrase to Capital: "History reveals no civilized people among whom there were not a highly educated class, and large aggregations of wealth, represented usually by the clergy and the nobility. Inspiration has always come from above. . . . Large profits mean large pay rolls. But profits must be the result of service performed. . . ."[1]

And then a word to Labor: "Statutes must appeal to more than material welfare. Wages won't satisfy, be they never so large. Nor houses; nor lands; nor coupons, though they fall thick as the leaves of autumn. Man has a spiritual nature. Touch it, and it must respond as the magnet responds to the pole. To that, not to selfishness, let the laws of the Commonwealth appeal. Recognize the immortal worth and dignity of man. Let the laws of Massachusetts proclaim to her humblest citizen, performing the most menial task,

[1] *Have Faith in Massachusetts.* Houghton Mifflin Company, 1919.

the recognition of his manhood, the recognition that
all men are peers, the humblest with the most exalted,
the recognition that all work is glorified."

But it was Mr. Coolidge's disquisition on the nature of politics that I sought most hopefully while
trying to find out and report about him. I looked to
see what he had to say about the office-holders and
found this: "But the fact remains that office brokerage
is here held in reprehensive scorn and professional
office-seeking in contempt. Every native-born American, however, is potentially a President, and it must
always be remembered that the obligation to serve
the State is forever binding upon all, although office is
the gift of the people. . . . Another reason why political life of this nature is not chosen as a career is
that it does not pay. . . . Few prominent members of
Congress are dependent on their salary, which is but
another way of saying that in Washington Senators
and Representatives need more than their official
salaries to become most effective.

". . . But I do not feel that there is any more obligation to run for office than there is to become a banker,
a merchant, a teacher, or enter any other special occupation. As indicated, some men have a particular
aptitude in this direction and some have none. Of
course experience counts here as in any other human
activity, and all experience worth the name is the result of application, of time and thought and study and
practice. If the individual finds he has liking and

capacity for this work, he will involuntarily find himself engaged in it. There is no catalogue of such capacity. One man gets results in one way, another in another. But in general only the man of broad sympathy and deep understanding of his fellow-men can meet with much success."

I won't pretend to discern an autobiographical note in that, though some persons gifted with quicker divination may. At any rate, no exception can be taken to it by even the most critical, nor of such pronouncements as these:

"We live under a republican form of government. We need forever to remember that representative government does represent. A careless, indifferent representative is the result of a careless, indifferent electorate."

"There are selfishness and injustice and evil in the world. . . ."

"There will come out of government exactly what is put into it."

"Society gets about what it deserves."

"Of course the present estimate is not the ultimate. There are men here who appear important that will not appear so in years to come."

The one personal reference I find in this discourse on politics is this: "Cannon has said of McKinley that his ear was so close to the ground that it was full of grasshoppers."

You will easily perceive that the Vice-President is

no trouble-maker. He does not introduce new and strange elements in an already disordered world. He clings fast to the established doctrine. He sings the old songs. He likes the familiar known things. In the old parliamentary phrase he calls for the regular order. He never does the unexpected or the surprising thing. He is not the first, or even the second or third, by whom the new is tried. His career in politics is proof that a substantial element among us approve just that sort of thing.

On the day of the first Cabinet meeting of the Harding administration all the newspaper correspondents in Washington, and apparently all the movie operators and camera men east of a line drawn north and south through Pittsburgh, attended at the executive offices to make a pictorial and descriptive record of the newcomers, for the enlightenment and education of the dear ones at home. The photographers ran as wild as deuces. They took pictures of the Cabinet members and the President, collectively and individually, indoors and outdoors, in motion and standing still, and finally a series of prints of the Cabinet in session. Mr. Coolidge sat with the Cabinet. It was an innovation. He was pictured in his place at the Cabinet table sitting with the others. When the meeting was over, the correspondent of the *Boston Transcript*, seeking a paragraph of local interest to enliven his dispatch, greeted the great man and asked:

"Mr. Vice-President, where did you sit at the Cabinet table? What place was allotted you in the order of precedence?"

Mr. Coolidge considered thoughtfully. He weighed the possibilities of any hasty speech. He thought deeply. Then he said, slowly:

"I had rather any announcement on that point should come directly from the President."

When he chooses he has the power of condensed epigrammatic expression. Take this bit, for example: "Do the day's work. If it be to protect the rights of the weak, whoever objects, do it. If it be to help a powerful corporation better to serve the people, whatever the opposition, do that. Expect to be called a stand-patter, but don't be a stand-patter. Expect to be called a demagogue, but don't be a demagogue. Don't hesitate to be as revolutionary as science. Don't hesitate to be as reactionary as the multiplication table. Don't expect to build up the weak by pulling down the strong. Don't hurry to legislate. Give administration a chance to catch up with legislation."

Before the microscopists at Washington are done with him, he will be catalogued and indexed and cross-referenced. He is under scrutiny. Before his term of office is over, though he may continue dumb as any oracle, he will be known, measured, weighed, appraised, and valued for what he is.

I know competent questers who are hot on the trail. For the present they make only provisional verdicts on this foster-child of Silence and slow Time. He is a type entirely new to Washington.

BRYAN: GAYLY THE TROUBADOUR

MR. BRYAN is one of the great troubadours, and as such I sing him. Never in our time was another such as he. Troubadouring is the thing he does best. It is really his vocation. He enjoys it. Faring forth with him among the constituencies is an experience full of lights and shadows and picturesque and dramatic incidents.

The open season for troubadours is in the two mellow months preceding the November presidential election. This is the time of the real singing. It is the time of "swinging around the circle." The candidates for the presidency have to go out and perform whether or not they are troubadours and have any love for it. Cox and Harding left no traditions. Neither Taft nor Wilson was a real troubadour. Bryan and Roosevelt were, and Bryan is the best of them all. He likes it all: the early rising, the crowded days, the bands, the turmoil, the shouting and applause. He doesn't mind the queer food, because he eats only milk toast in towns that don't have a first-class presidential postmaster. He can sleep anywhere and at any time. Therefore, it used to seem odd, to one who knew his backgrounds, to see Mr. Bryan sitting in the State Department in an environment of braided one-button morning coats, and an atmosphere of burning sealing wax suggesting secrecy. Somehow he didn't seem to fit into the picture.

WILLIAM JENNINGS BRYAN

Quite aside from the desire to make money, Mr. Bryan's appearances on the Chautauqua circuit after he became Secretary of State came from a liking for that sort of thing. The general criticism at that time was that it was a pretty poor sort of business for a Secretary of State ; but that aspect of the affair did not mean anything to Mr. Bryan. His habits are fixed, and one of them is to speak at Chautauquas. He would probably have done the same had he been President. One of the things Mr. Bryan's critics do not understand is that all of his broad experience and the changes in his personal fortunes have not affected any of the essential qualities of his character. In his daily walk and habits he is the same man now that he was twenty-five years ago. Being Secretary of State made no difference to him. He could not understand that as Secretary of State he could not say and do things that he had been doing without public criticism all the years. It was an impropriety for a Secretary of State to appear on the platform the same evening with itinerant troupes of entertainers. It had never been accounted an impropriety for W. J. Bryan, private citizen, to appear in such an environment. Mr. Bryan made no distinction.

Let me begin at the beginning and attempt to tell the story of a day, which began at one o'clock on an October morning at Lincoln, and ended at eleven o'clock that night when the train pulled out from Cedar Rapids for Chicago. The Peerless Leader made fifteen speeches in that interval and shook hands with many thousands of admiring farmers and railroad shop men.

Mr. Bryan spoke the preceding night at Havelock to a throng of railway employees. It was cold and raw and drizzling, and the black mud was sticky underfoot. He got back into Lincoln, very hoarse, on a trolley car, about midnight, and had supper up in Frank Richards's rooms, with the five correspondents who were traveling with him and his secretary, Bob Rose. Richards was the proprietor of the hotel at Lincoln. The cold fried chicken, the sliced tomatoes, and the bread-and-butter sandwiches were finished, and the party came downstairs to find the streets shrouded in a heavy fog. We were supposed to be on our way to Des Moines and bought tickets for that point. There were twenty or more men on the platform of the little station. Most of them shook hands with Mr. Bryan before the train came in, a few minutes before one o'clock.

The sleeping-car porter waked the members of Mr. Bryan's party soon after six o'clock that morning and they were in various stages of undress when the train arrived at Valley Junction, an indeterminate sort of little town five miles below Des Moines. Mr. Bryan had his face covered with lather, preparatory to shaving. Some of the other members of the party were just climbing sleepily out of their upper berths. Early as was the hour, two or three hundred people were at the station, and the Local Committee clamored for admission. Bob Rose went out to the platform to explain.

"Mr. Bryan is dressing and is sorry that he cannot come out and see you all," he said.

"But he is scheduled to make a speech here. We have all come down to meet him. There is a big crowd up the street waiting," was the amazing reply.

Neither Mr. Bryan nor any of his party had been notified of this engagement, but the Peerless Leader hastily washed the lather off his face, dressed and got off the train. The laggard members of his party followed him, collarless and in their shirt-sleeves, and completed their toilet on the station platform, in the presence of the amused and gaping crowd. The procession started on foot up Main Street, headed by the Valley Junction Silver Cornet Band, consisting of two fifes and a drum.

The first stop was at "Hy" Drexel's café for breakfast. The doors were closed to all except the members of Mr. Bryan's party, while the populace pressed their noses to the pane at the front windows, watching the great man and his flying squadron eat an excellent breakfast of ham and eggs, lamb chops, and sliced oranges. The Peerless Leader consumed two cavernous bowls of milk toast.

From this oasis the line of march led a block west and half a block north to a vacant lot adjoining the City Hall. The fire department occupied the ground floor of the municipal building, and on the side of it facing the vacant lot was painted an advertisement for a real Havana five-cent cigar. "Cap" de Ford introduced Mr. Bryan to the thousand or more people who crowded about the stand. While waiting for the "Cap" to conclude his introduction, one somehow found oneself feeling sorry for Mr. Bryan. One involuntarily recalled other days, and remembered other scenes; of tired actors waiting in the old car shed at Atlanta, Georgia, for the early morning train to Birmingham. The whole present performance seemed so abnormal. The environment evidently depressed Mr. Bryan, too, for he preached to his audience, scarcely talking politics at all.

The crowd followed Mr. Bryan to the station, and some girls sang campaign songs until he got on the rear day coach of a local train to go to Perry, where he was scheduled to speak at noon.

At every stop Mr. Bryan made a rear-platform speech to shouting, enthusiastic crowds of farmers, their wives and children. The rear coach became crowded to the point of suffocation. At every stop the passengers in the forward coaches who had not contrived to squeeze into Mr. Bryan's coach got off the train and ran back to the tail end to hear the speeches. At the warning cry, "All aboard!" they would make a dash for the train. The man in charge of the baggage car came back to hear every speech between Valley Junction and Perry, running the entire length of the train twice each time. He must have done sixty-three miles before noon.

In these rear-platform speeches Mr. Bryan freely

used Biblical quotations and allusions. Every time he made use of one the crowd shouted with enthusiastic approval. It is difficult to imagine a more effective oratorical style than Mr. Bryan employs in these speeches. It is intimate, easy, and colloquial, and makes instant appeal to his audiences. His sentences are short and ordinarily he employs words of not more than two syllables. He has acquired the rare art of condensation and can say a great deal in a brief space of time. He drives his point home. He understands his audiences from the ground up. Their mode of life and their thoughts are as familiar to him as his own. There can be no manner of doubt that he "gets next" to the people.

All day long men came up to Mr. Bryan renewing old acquaintance, and the last thing one heard that night from an upper berth, as Mr. Bryan was crawling into a lower one, was a whiskered individual saying: "You know me, Mr. Bryan. I am old man Mullens' son — J. P. Mullens is my name. You remember when you was up to our town there was a big crowd of people in the street, and I stuck my head out of the window and yelled 'Hooray for Bryan'; and you looked up at me and waved your hand. I'm that very fellow."

Of course Mr. Bryan remembered him. He remembers all the various and sundry individuals that come to him with the same formula: "You remember me? I'm the man,—"

Possibly the most illuminating incident of the whole

day came near Tama. Mr. Bryan had gone forward into the washroom of the car to get the deferred shave of which he stood in need. He had just finished and was standing coatless and collarless, with a towel stuck in his neckband to protect his shirt-front, when the train stopped for a moment at a little station just outside of Tama. Mr. Bryan had not had time to wash the remaining flecks of lather from his face. The people outside were calling for him. A half-dozen men and some dear old ladies in sunbonnets were running alongside of the car calling up: "Is Mr. Bryan in there?"

The Peerless Leader responded: "Yes, but I'm shaving and can't come out."

"Well, stick your head out of the window and let us have a look at you, anyway."

Mr. Bryan pulled the towel from his neckband and thrust his head and the upper part of his body out of the window, all in undress as he was, and grasped the hands that were reached up to him.

Neither he nor the people outside seemed to think there was anything unusual in the performance. It was not undignified. It was just friendly and simple, and lacking in all pretense. Neither the men nor the women who wanted to shake hands with Mr. Bryan were "shocked" at seeing him without coat, waistcoat, or collar, and with face unwashed after shaving.

Now that is the sort of a day that Mr. Bryan likes. He turned in as fresh as a daisy that night and beaming with happiness. No concourse of ambassadors, however splendiferous, no Washington company, however brilliant, and no mere "desk job," however distinguished, could compensate Mr. Bryan for continued absence from these beloved scenes. For his is the singing heart of the real troubadour. He cannot withstand its calling.

I recall and recapture another scene.

When the Democrats sit formally at meat, they insist, quite in the old spacious way, on having their troubadours, minnesingers, and jongleurs about them. They love their sweet singers. They love the words and music. They set their course by sweet melody. They derive inspiration and moral sustenance from all their silver-tongued.

After all, there is an ineradicable and fundamental difference between a Democrat and a Republican. It goes deeper than any difference over political and campaign issues. It is a difference of temperament, of habit, of thought, of attitude, and outlook on life. It is never so sharply and clearly revealed as at their conventions and their national committee meetings.

The Democratic National Committee was called to meet at Washington to select a place of meeting for the national convention and, following the usual custom, gave a dinner in the evening, which the Democrats prefer to call a "banquet." It befell as ordered, but, in order to accommodate all of the multitude, melody-thirsty and music-loving, two dinners had to be held simulta-

neously in two hotels, with a "staggered" list of twelve
speakers. As soon as a speaker had finished at one
banquet, he was hastened to the other to repeat his
performance. Thus it came about that these devoted
people sat under a steady deluge and torrent of oratory
from eight o'clock in the evening until close on to three
o'clock the following morning. During this whole time
they sat under a roaring torrent and downpour of more
or less incandescent words. And the incredible fact is
to be recorded that they left refreshed and stimulated.

All the famous troubadours of the party came from
far and near. Of these Mr. Bryan is easily the chief.
Like that other great singer who preceded him in the
golden age of the troubadours, Raimbaut d'Aurenga,
he could describe himself as "young-hearted, fresh,
and in perfect health"; and I for one found him hard
to resist when he bade the jongleurs strike up a lively
air and began his latest song:

> With wits refreshed and fresh desire,
> With knowledge fresh and freshened fire,
> In fine fresh style, that ne'er will tire,
> A good fresh poem I'll begin;
> My fresh new verses will inspire
> Fresh life in every knight and squire,
> And freshen pulses old and thin!

As he stood there in the eddying tobacco smoke, facing a none too friendly crowd, I, his detached and long-
time chronicler, knew that he meant to fare forth again
among the constituencies and hoped that again I might
be with him. Like Cœur de Lion, he is a born traveler.

He finds refreshment and uplift in wayfaring along the open road ; in the roar and bustle of arrival and departure at small towns where his coming and going is an event ; the applause of friendly audiences, and the freedom from restraint.

The world, as is well known, goes round and round, and thus it comes about that all sorts of things recur. The Marquis Albert of Malaspina, back in the golden ages, publicly taunted the great Raimbaut : "Tell me, Raimbaut, if it please you : Is it a fact that the lady you have been singing so much to has jilted you, as people say?" And Raimbaut was able to sing : "Though love desert me, I will achieve all the good I can ; though I lose my lady, I will not lose my fame and talent" ; and he sang again of his future and the battles to come :

> In heat and cold, to come and go,
>   To trot and gallop, run and leap,
>   To toil and suffer, scarce to sleep, —
> This is the life I'm now to know;
> My inn the roadside or the grove at best,
> With iron and steel and ashen spear oppressed,
> With stern sirvente instead of love and song,
> The weak will I defend against the strong.

His voice was as limpid and as melodic as ever. He had had a hair-cut before dinner and his locks no longer curled upward at the ends. It made him look younger. He made the "parade" of candidates look thin and unreal. He dominated the whole gathering of the Democrats.

Now who do you suppose said this about our hero? "Not only have Mr. Bryan's character, his justice, his sincerity, his transparent integrity, his Christian principle, made a deep impression upon all with whom he has dealt; but his tact in dealing with men of many sorts, his capacity for business, his mastery of the principle of each matter he has been called upon to deal with, have cleared away many a difficulty....I cannot say what pleasure and profit I, myself, have taken from close association with Mr. Bryan or how thoroughly he has seemed to all of us who are associated with him here to deserve not only our confidence, but our affectionate admiration."

That was the testimony of Mr. Woodrow Wilson, who did not bestow his commendation lightly. No more reserved, no more cautious, no more reticent, no man with so much of the Scotch quality of canniness, has lived in the White House in the lifetime of this generation.

So far as is ascertainable to the lay student of Mr. Wilson's mental reaches and their tributaries, bayous, and lagoons, he never changed his mind about anything, except the initiative and referendum and William J. Bryan, since he became a grown man and began to have matured convictions and opinions. He became a convert to both these great natural forces in political life after coming into contact with their workings. He discovered the virtues of the initiative and referendum when he went out into the Northwest and visited Oregon and Washington. Mr. Bryan was rather wished on Mr. Wilson by the severe and inexorable logic of the political situation growing out of the Baltimore convention. After Mr. Wilson was elected there was nothing for it but to make Mr. Bryan Secretary of State.

Mr. Bryan's competency, his ability, his conduct as the head of our Department of Foreign Affairs, his appointments to the diplomatic corps and his efficiency as an administrator of departmental business and routine, are not under scrutiny here. Being Secretary of State was in the beginning the smallest part of Mr. Bryan's business and the least important aspect of his value to the Wilson administration. He will not rank with Madison, Monroe, Daniel Webster, John Hay, or Elihu Root as a Secretary of State. His dispatches will not be used in after years as models for aspiring young diplomatists. But his usefulness was in no way abated by his failure to rise to the heights of some of his famous predecessors in the Department of State. Mr. Bryan was indispensable to Mr. Wilson in the making of the Tariff Bill and the Currency Bill. Everybody remarked about the Currency Bill that the wonder was, not that so much that was good was put into it, but that so much that was bad was kept out of it. Much of the keeping out was Mr. Bryan's work.

Mr. Bryan subdued the heathen that imagine vain things. And he did it all quietly and without seeking to make himself appear a moving factor in the situation.

As persons know who were in Washington through the first summer of the Wilson régime, when the Tariff Bill and the Currency Bill were in the making, Mr. Bryan's ante-room was crowded day by day with members and with others from the hinterland, eager for a sign. They wanted Mr. Bryan to give the bills his blessing. They wanted to know about this and that provision. Mr. Bryan talked with all of them and told them what they came to find out. They could not all see Mr. Wilson, and most of them would have been extremely uncomfortable in his presence, but they felt they knew Bryan. He belonged to their tribe and talked their language. They had been to the wars together before.

Washington, for the most part, wholly misapprehended Mr. Bryan. It regarded him solely as Secretary of State and applied to him the standards of conduct and deportment that have come to be regarded as standards of that office. Social Washington and much of political Washington did not know of Mr. Bryan's activities outside of the State Department. They heard of his simple friendliness and the informality of his discourse with diplomats, and, having artificial standards and perhaps in many instances false standards, they were made ashamed. I found that the sneers at Mr. Bryan were by no means reflected by the understanding members of the diplomatic corps stationed here. Some of the ambassadors rather went out of the way to express their admiration of Mr. Bryan's simplicity, of his absolute candor, of the sincerity he showed in official intercourse. They saw that he was a dreamer, an idealist; that his heart runs away with his head; that he was lacking in guile; that he spoke to them truthfully; and these qualities they appreciated because they are so rare in their experience with more sophisticated foreign offices.

Mr. Bryan came to the office too late in life to acquire reputation as a great Department chief, as an administrator and an executive. He depended too much on inspiration. He saw too many people to allow him the proper time to attend to the details of his office. Prior to being Secretary of State he had never had any executive experience. Every office of foreign affairs is a hive of concrete details, of precedents. Almost every case that comes up has a history. Present decisions are influenced and limited and to a degree determined by a policy laid down by some other Secretary of State who may have been dead a quarter of a century. Mr. Bryan did not withhold the time to himself to withdraw from the daily hurly-burly and coolly review and master the essentials of important problems that confronted his Department. It is revealing no secret to say that President Wilson did that for him.

Mr. Bryan winced and became restive under the criticism he received. Some of it cut him to the quick. The continued charges that he was unable to comprehend the business of the State Department, that he did not know what was going on under his nose, that he did not read the dispatches, and that, reading them, he could not understand them, particularly hurt Mr. Bryan. He resented this criticism far more than the popular disapproval that was visited upon his diplomatic appointments. On the face of it, it seems probable that Mr. Wilson knew of Mr. Bryan's state of mind and sought to alleviate his mortification when he wrote a letter giving specific commendation to Mr. Bryan's capacity for business, he having "given to the policy of the State Department a definiteness and dignity that are very admirable." This was by no means the Washington verdict on Mr. Bryan's first year in office, but it was Mr. Wilson's, and there was no occasion for him to say it unless he chose to say it.

Anyhow, Mr. Bryan was as useful and effective as any Secretary of State that Mr. Wilson had during his eight years. That, I concede, is not saying much. In office Mr. Bryan is a caged bird and can't sing. And he must sing. For he is a true troubadour and not a double-entry bookkeeper.

JOHNSON: A HERALD WITH TRUMPET

IN our time there have been just three national political leaders; true, natural leaders not dependent upon organizations or the political situation, or (as they are called), issues; who made their own issues as the season and the opportunity offered. I mean men with national personal followings. Men who could command an appreciable number of votes on any national question on whatever side they chose to take.

You can have no doubt about their identity: William J. Bryan, Theodore Roosevelt, Woodrow Wilson. Can you think of another since Grover Cleveland, and, before Cleveland, Abraham Lincoln? Would you include Ulysses S. Grant? I would not.

Indeed, I suspect there are those who are doubtful about the rightful inclusion of Mr. Wilson. He came to his authority and leadership in the presidency. It was not a natural growth. Being in the White House was a tremendous accessory to the fact. But he must be included by courtesy if not by right. Roosevelt was helped, too, by being President, but not enough to impair the validity of his natural leadership, and he did not lose his personal following when he lost office. There can be no manner of doubt about Bryan. The "Bryan vote" from 1896 to 1912 was as solid, as patent, as obvious, as overwhelming a factor in politics as existed in this land. It had to be reckoned with and taken into account.

Now, Hiram Johnson bids fair to join the ranks of these three and become a recognized national political leader with a clearly defined personal following. The Johnson vote is smaller and less compact and less a factor, but it exists, though to a degree formless and still in the making. Both Johnson and Bryan derive whatever power and authority they possess directly from the electors without the aid of any intermediaries or organization. Their followings are a natural growth, first acquired and then cultivated. They have gone directly to first sources for their warrant of authority. They have each sought to be President, and, while their method of approach has been the same and placed on the same general plan of direct appeal, their execution and technique have been wholly unlike.

If Mr. Bryan is a troubadour and a silver tongue, Mr. Johnson is a herald with a trumpet. He is militant. He summons to arms. He blows a blast outside the walls of Jericho, and if the walls do not fall he uses a battering-ram. Like any knight errant he is always ready to tilt a joust against any one who does not measure up to his ideas of a champion of the public weal.

Hiram Johnson is a bold, forthright questing man. He wants to be President of the United States. He believes he has the courage, the intelligence, the experience, the qualities of mind and character — the general fitness to be the Chief Executive of this nation.

SENATOR HIRAM W. JOHNSON

His problem is to find out how many of us agree with him. He offered himself for the nomination in 1920 and failed.

Being nominated for President and being elected President are two totally different processes. The nomination is controlled in great degree by the party organization. The election is decided by popular vote. To be nominated a candidate must have an organization of his own and plenty of money to spend. Delegate-hunting as practiced among us is the most costly of all outdoor sports.

The presidential primaries in some of the States have made possible such lone-hand candidacies as Hiram Johnson's. State primary laws made possible his two elections as Governor and his choice as Senator from California. These same laws make possible for him another trial for the presidency. The campaign of 1920 was Johnson's first defeat at the head of a ticket. My own guess is that he will not accept that verdict as final.

Now what sort of a man is this Hiram Warren Johnson? Let's walk up close and look at him. I went to California on this quest. I sought the verdict of the vicinage. If the people of his native State were not for him, I knew he had no chance of impressing himself on the nation. It may be said at once that California supports Johnson. The State believes in him.

In my innocence I thought it would be a simple thing to draw a picture of Hiram Johnson. Here, one

said to oneself, is a big, breezy, colorful, picturesque
personality against a Western background. He must
figure in scores of good anecdotes. It will be as easy to
write about him as it would be about T. R. All one has
to do is to go out and get it. Even arriving at Sacramento on a rainy Sunday did not blur these bright
imaginings. Then to the telephone only to discover
that Johnson was in San Francisco. Oh, well, it is a
rainy day and we will make a start bright and early
Monday morning.

Monday morning. Now for the flying start. We are
in the back room of Colonel Snook's real estate office.
The doors are closed, but not before the Colonel had
told the boy outside to "tell 'em all I'm out." Business
of lighting cigars and settling down for a closed session.
"Now, tell me all about Johnson. What sort of a fellow he is. Everything you know about him."

The Colonel and Johnson went to school together.
They have been close friends ever since they were
seven or eight years old. But Colonel Snook was
Number One on the list of inarticulate emotionalists
belonging to the great Johnson-I-Knew-Him-When
Club in California. He got under way slowly.

"Well," he said, "Johnson is certainly the best two-
fisted fighting man I ever knew. He is a real scrapper.
He certainly has run true to form. There is a man who
won't look for trouble, but who never dodges it. But
you ought to talk to a friend of his down in San Francisco. He is a lawyer down there. I'll give you his

name. He knows a lot about Johnson. Or you ought to go over to the City Library and talk to Ripley, who was in school with the Governor and who ought to have some good stories. Come back and see me again. Maybe I'll think of something."

And now to the Library to see Mr. Ripley: "Yes, I have known the Governor ever since he was a boy. He used to live in the house right across the street there. He certainly is a fighter. I do not mean that he is a bully or seeks trouble, but he was always willing to fight. He is just the same as a man that he was as a boy."

"Yes," one added persuasively; "you must know a lot of good stories about him. Tell them to me."

"I think you had better go over to the 'Bee' office and talk with the editor. He ought to be able to tell you lots of things that would be interesting."

Three blocks down the main street, two blocks to the right, up the stairs, and one finds the young lady at the switchboard in the Sacramento "Bee" office. "Is the editor in?" one asked in the Eastern voice. "Do you mean C. K.?" said the damsel brightly. "I think he's at home. I will ring him up and see." She punched at the switchboard, as they do, and presently asked: "Is C. K. there?" He was, but before one went out to see him one ventured to ask: "Why do you call him C. K.?"

"Because that is his name," she said; but the question puzzled her.

C. K. began: "He certainly is a good fighting man. Johnson never was afraid of a scrap."

"How about a good anecdote or two?"

"Well, have you seen Colonel Snook or Ripley over at the Library?"

The circle was complete. It was time for lunch. One had received the fixed impression that Johnson was a fighter. Conceive this process repeated again and again, until one of Johnson's bitterest opponents gave the sought-for clue. The query was put this way: "What about Johnson? He seems to be able to put over almost anything in this State. How does he get away with it?"

"Well, I will tell you. He certainly is one of the best fight —"

"Yes, yes," one interrupted, "that is established. But isn't there anything else to him?"

"Well"— slowly —"when he says he is going to do a thing he does it. When he starts out on anything he never lets go until he carries it through. When he makes a promise he keeps it. He has kept every promise he has made to the people of this State. He has done everything that he told them he would do, and now they trust him and believe in him absolutely."

That gave me a basis, so I went to the Senator from California to find out what he thought about himself.

He has a square jaw and a clear, gray eye. It is full of light and fire and vigor. His hair, too, is gray, and he has plenty of it. It is stiff and short and always stays parted. There is nothing breezy, colorful, or picturesque about him ; nothing high, wide, and care-less. He is just serious and purposeful.

Johnson told me at once : "If you are going to write about me, you won't have to go back of 1910. Before that time I was either in school or wearing a path between my house and my office. I spent my days at my desk or in the courts, and when I got through work in the afternoon I went home and stayed until it was time to go to work again next morning. The years since 1910 are all of my life. My real life began when I was given an opportunity to quit working for myself and begin working for the people of the State."

But before I get down to the business of disclosing the basis on which Johnson has erected himself and become in turn Governor, United States Senator, and presidential possibility, I must tell the one Hiram Johnson anecdote in existence. For I found it at last. I pass it on as I received it. Whether it is told by the oldest inhabitant or the youngest reporter I cannot determine. The narrative styles of the two are so alike. But I found it in the Sacramento "Bee" of November 7, 1916. Here it is :

"Do you remember the time when General Grant visited Sacramento on his return from a trip around the world and was given a great ovation in front of the State Capitol?"

"The address of welcome was delivered by Henry Edgerton, the grandest orator of his day, whose eloquent recital of the General's life calls to mind the subsequent but no more magnificent epitome of the career of Napoleon by Robert Ingersoll.

"Grant and W. H. Mills visited school, and the teachers were in a quandary about a proper welcome.

"All but one threw up their hands in despair, declaring they had no pupil prepared for such an emergency. That one was Miss Jessie McMenomy, of the Sacramento Grammar School, now Mrs. N. E. White.

"'I have a lad in my class,' said she, 'who can always be depended on to meet an emergency. Hiram Johnson is not afraid to face the great man.'

"And do you remember how the world's great military chieftain — stolid though his nature — displayed much difficulty in suppressing his emotion during young Hiram's spirited recital of 'Sheridan's Ride,' and how his voice trembled as he openly complimented the lad on his forensic ability?

"'Hiram,' said his teacher as the former returned to his seat, 'I prophesy there are many here to-day who will yet see you standing in General Grant's shoes.'

"And that prophecy bids fair to be realized."

Read it over again. It is a perfect model. It rigidly conforms to every convention. I cannot for a moment accept Senator Johnson's disclaimer that it is not true; that he never made a speech to General Grant. Besides, he is the only person I could find in Sacramento who didn't believe the story, and if it is not true it ought to be.

Johnson is bursting with energy and vitality; he is always under high pressure; he is dominant, masterful, impatient of restraint, demandful for what he believes to be right; "a born leader," as the dear old phrase has it. He is pugnacious, always a fighter, and incapable of using "moral suasion." Finally, he is as independent as a wood sawyer's clerk. As might be expected with these qualities, he is a good hater. You are either his friend or his enemy. There is no middle ground. The people of California, among whom he has lived all his life, either praise him to the skies or denounce him in terms that if printed would scorch the begonias.

Hiram Johnson is a Native Son. He was born at Sacramento, September 2, 1866, and educated in the public schools there. He was twelve years old when he told General Grant how Sheridan saved the day by coming up from Winchester twenty miles away, and he was seventeen years old when he was graduated from the Sacramento High School. He learned shorthand and spent a year in his father's law office as a stenographer. At eighteen he entered the University of California in the Class of '88, but left in the middle of his junior year to marry. He was then just twenty years old.

From the time he was married until he was thirty-six years old Johnson practiced law in Sacramento with his father and his brother Albert. He was interested in politics and for a time was city attorney. In the hope of increasing his practice and his income, Johnson removed to San Francisco in 1902 with his brother. They soon dissolved partnership and Hiram went it alone. He seems to get on better that way. He established a successful practice in San Francisco. He was called one of the best jury lawyers on the Pacific Coast.

Johnson has one outstanding endearing quality. He doesn't value money. "Why, if we didn't watch him," one of his associates told me, "he would start East with only six dollars in his pocket." Simply he looks upon money as a medium of exchange, and not as something to be hoarded and sweated over. His personal habits are of the simplest. He spends his evenings at home or at the movie shows. He is perhaps the most inveterate movie fan in the country to-day. He knows the names of all the movie actors and actresses, and can tell you what parts they have played.

He told me that he started going to the movies as a refuge. The picture theaters being dark, he could spend an hour or two without being seen and pestered. They offered a means of escape from importunities. But now he goes to them because he likes them. Also, he is a domino-player of renown — "the best domino-player in the world," a Sacramento friend told me gravely.

Johnson was not associated with the beginning of the reform movement in California. He was practicing law in San Francisco when it began. Prior to 1910 California was in an evil plight — machine-ridden. The fight to free the State began with a group of men in municipal elections in the south. The first real advance was made when a direct primary law was passed. This gave the little group of men who had organized to lift California out of the mire their opportunity. They cast about for a fighter to lead their cause. They wanted a man of fire, of energy, with clean hands, and free from entangling alliances, who could make an appeal direct to the people. They decided that Johnson was such a man. The moral impulse in his character had led him to take a vigorous interest in public affairs. He was a man who took fire at an idea. He had made himself known all over the State by his participation in the graft cases. He was sought out and solicited to run as Republican candidate for Governor at the August, 1910, primaries. The so-called Lincoln-Roosevelt Republican League was organized to endorse his candidacy. After some hesitation, Johnson accepted. That was his start. Since that he has been twice elected Governor and once United States Senator, each time by largely increased pluralities, and has been a candidate for Vice-President of the United States, and finally a strong contender for nomination for the presidency. Certainly an astonishing eleven-year record.

Now you know as much about him as I do. He is a man of quick sympathies and sensitive to praise or blame. Politicians should have thick hides to be at ease. Johnson is not pachydermatous. He is sensitive, he is modest, and he is diffident. He can be quickly inflamed. He is just fifty-five years old now and in the prime of his vigor. What he will make of himself in the coming ten years is one of the interesting speculations in our national politics.

I don't think he will ever settle down to a routine. Not, at any rate, while his emotions are so quickly alive and he is so ready to throw himself into any fray where the issue appeals to his sense of justice. He is not a canny or a cautious or a moderate man. And looking, I suspect, is the thing he would think least about before leaping.

Whether he can find a national market for his political product, I don't know. Colonel Roosevelt, who was one of the shrewdest politicians, sensed this defect and touched upon it lightly in a letter he wrote in 1916. He said: "I genuinely believe that if the East could understand Johnson, we could get the Republicans to nominate him; but, good Lord, we are a parochial people, and it is the hardest thing in the world to get the people of one section, whether it is the Mississippi Valley or the Rocky Mountains States or the Middle West or the East, really to understand what another section such as the Coast is doing. Indeed, it is not too easy to get Oregon and Washington to understand what California is doing."

If Johnson can impress himself upon the East as he has upon California the rest will be easy, but until he does —

LOST IN THE MISTS

CONCEIVE, if you will, the Honorable Bourke Cockran, freshly come again to the House after a long absence, rising in his place on a hot summer afternoon and making sonorous lamentation :

"How many of the members around me now are known to the country at large ? I repeat this question with mournful realization that the answer cannot inspire us with pride in the situation."

The experienced old silver-tongue with a sure instinct had hit upon the one topic that members of Congress never tire of talking about. They listened while he recited the story of their wrongs. Let us, too, draw near the lodge of sorrow and hear him booming his doleful cadences :

"When I came to this House in the Fiftieth Congress reports and descriptions of our proceedings occupied the front page of every newspaper in America. When I returned to the Fifty-Eighth Congress, after an absence of eight years, I found that the space allotted to us in the newspapers had shrunk to about a column. I return now, after an absence of twelve years, and find we have no place at all. Accounts of our proceedings are not accorded in the newspapers to-day as much space as a ball given by a fashionable woman.

"Recall to mind the names of a few among the

men who were conspicuous in the Fiftieth Congress, and who would not, I believe, have exchanged their prominence here for any other place in the whole world? — John G. Carlisle, Roger Q. Mills, the two Breckinridges, William L. Wilson, Benton McMillan, on this side. On that side, Thomas B. Reed. I may mention also William McKinley. And I could run through a long list of names famous in our history.

"Why has this House shrunk so low in public esteem? Why are our proceedings no longer important enough to obtain even mention in the newspapers? Why are gentlemen, as soon as they reach a conspicuous place here, ready to give up that which formerly was the dearest aspiration of genius and patriotism in order to seek elsewhere success which they consider more valuable and more creditable?

"It was upon this floor and in this House that the reputations were established of the greatest political leaders in our history. Not one was ever established in the Senate. Not in the Senate, but in the House, did Henry Clay win the renown upon which his authority rested. Here also did James G. Blaine acquire the popularity which made mention of his name in any Republican gathering an occasion for demonstration of affection that was absolutely rapturous.

"Neither Blaine nor Clay ever succeeded in reaching the Presidency, but they remained, while they lived, the idols, objects of adoration to their respective parties, embracing nearly one half of the people. I myself saw and heard William J. Bryan emerge by a single speech on the floor from the position of a new and unknown member to a degree of prominence which led to his nomination three times for the Presidency and to the domination of his party for twenty years.

"Why are no successors to these giants produced by our proceedings now? What is it that has atrophied this House — reduced it to such sterility? I have heard it said that the reason for this decline of the House in importance is a decline in the ability of its members. Nothing, in my judgment, could be further from the truth. I have known the House for thirty-four years, and now on my return, after an absence of twelve years, I have been profoundly impressed and immensely cheered by the high order of ability displayed in debate on this floor.

"The Senate has become all-powerful. The House has declined till it is a negligible quantity. Is this an exaggeration? What effect have you on public opinion to-day? These speeches which are of the highest excellence — which in other days would have been widely read — are nowhere reported. Not even the fact that they were delivered is mentioned in the newspaper press.

"And why should it be otherwise under existing conditions — conditions of your own creation — for which you yourselves are responsible? By rules and by procedure which you have sanctioned you have renounced and thrown away the power which the Constitution conferred upon you and upon which your consequence depended."

And so on and so on and so on. Ever since I have known the House, it has been asking, why aren't we known, why aren't our speeches printed, why can't we be great men, too, like the giants of other days? And every so often the project revives for a Government newspaper that will print the speeches and debates, but nothing comes of it. Ten days after Bourke Cockran's speech, Albert Johnson, of Washington, who used to be a reporter, recurred to the subject and suggested that many an American schoolboy, if asked to define the function of the Roman Senate, would be tempted to reply that the institution existed for the purpose of listening to the speeches of Cicero. "Perhaps," he added, "that is what Cicero himself thought." Mr. Johnson thought the House was a more efficient legislative body because by shutting off the stream of talk the members have been able to perform their proper functions as a great governing body. He conceded that the orators enjoyed the mellifluous sound of their own voices, but said bluntly enough that they were no help to business.

Whatever the cause, it remains true enough that few men in the House enjoy a national reputation, and that a man can be a member of Congress for years and years, attending faithfully to his business, and never become known outside of his district, or, at most, his State. They all may have been useful, effective members of the House, each in his own way, without ever having acquired fame or a wide reputation.

Fifty-six members of the present House have served from seven to twenty-three two-year terms; that is, from fourteen to forty-six years. They have been continuously under public scrutiny and observation. How many of them do you know? How many of them can you even name? The House is a great bulk of unknown figures.

In every country in the world — except ours — where parliamentary government is enjoyed, the war has brought to the fore in the popular assemblies new men, new figures, new political elements, new groups representing new ideas, while we alone have reached back to the old standpat days — what the politicians now think of as the Dark Ages of our domestic concerns — and resuscitated a group of conservative veterans. They represent, even in the estimation of their own colleagues and party, an ancient order of things.

I stress their present eminence because this new country presents at this moment parliamentary leaders so different from the men who will frame legislation in the old countries. In common with other democracies we have a strong liking for the rule of seniority and order of precedence. There is nothing I can say in its favor. It is responsible for the present organization in the House. It is responsible for the lack of new figures and new blood at the top. It enables a dull and mediocre Congressman, coming from a "safe district," to remain in Washington year after year, to rise by inevitable processes to a place of power and authority and command. It made Mr. Claude Kitchin, of Scotland Neck, North Carolina, Chairman of the Committee on Ways and Means, just as, in due course, it has made Mr. Fordney, of Michigan, his successor.

Even Mr. Gillett, of Massachusetts, the Speaker, who came to the chair following a protest and insurrection on the part of the Republicans in the House against naming Mr. Mann for that honor, could not be called radical or restless or be accused of deeply yearning for a new order by even the most vivid imagination. An upright and able man, a politician against whom no charge of lack of interest in his country's welfare can be brought, he is of the eminently conservative and safe and sane type. He never shared or participated or aligned himself in sympathy or in action with the "insurgent group" in the Republican Party that first dethroned Cannon, the Speaker, in the House and at the same time pruned the speakership of its powers, nor was he in open sympathy or alliance with the little group of five so-called "progressive" Senators who protested so courageously and with such political effect against the Payne-Aldrich tariff bill. Through all the years, Mr. Gillett has been a regular Republican.

The blessed rule of seniority is responsible for the eminence of the present House leaders. There is nothing to be said in its favor. The House of Representatives does its business through committees. Members of the House attain rank and power and influence and position in the organization of that body through the character of their committee assignments. What may be called the "good" or important committees are those of Ways and Means, which frames tariff bills and other revenue measures; Appropriations, which has to do with disbursements of public moneys from the Treasury; Military Affairs, Naval Affairs, Judiciary, Agriculture, Post-Office and Post-Roads, Public Buildings and Grounds, Rivers and Harbors, and Interstate and Foreign Commerce. To come to occupy a ranking and powerful position, to become chairman of one of these committees, a member of the House has so to contrive his affairs at home in his own district that he remains continuously in Congress.

Mr. Gillett, Speaker, has been in Congress thirteen continuous terms. The revolt that made him Speaker was, therefore, not a violent break with tradition. Mr. Mann has been in the House eleven continuous terms. Mr. Mondell has also been a member for eleven terms, but not continuously, as he was not a member of the Fifty-Fifth Congress. Joseph W. Fordney, of Michigan, now Chairman of the Ways and Means Committee, has been in Congress for ten continuous terms. Philip Pitt Campbell, of Kansas, who is Chairman of the Rules Committee, has been in the House eight continuous terms.

The point I am making is that while under the present system the political color of the House may change from time to time, the quality of its dominant personnel is not greatly disturbed or altered. Before each Congressional election it is fairly well known who will occupy the chief positions in the House organization if the Democrats win and who will be the "leaders" if the Republicans are successful. That condition may have something to do with the present estate of the so-called popular branch. Really able and forceful and vigorous men are not willing to serve in the ruck for a long period of years before breaking through the thick crust of seniority. The country outside the House offers too many opportunities for advancement and preferment for a man of action and ability. Men of energy and substance do not want to stand in a long queue waiting for the gates of opportunity to open when other chances are immediately open to them elsewhere.

The House ought to command the best ability in this country, but notoriously it does not. There are able men in the House among its unknowns, and they will wait a long time before they become known. Long waiting too often dulls the edge of ambition. Men come to the House keen and alert and eager who after twenty years' service find themselves much like their fellows. They conform to the traditions, the practice and the spirit of the House.

And yet, after all, the House of Representatives is

representative. It keeps pace with the country. Its average of intelligence is the average of intelligence over our continent. We make it just what it is. Every two years we have a chance to throw out every man in it and put in new blood. If the people in Mr. Cannon's district and Mr. Fordney's and Mr. Mondell's and Mr. Garner's and Mr. Campbell's want these gentlemen to represent them term after term, they have a perfect right to choose them. But the result of this seniority bloc is that the House has small allure for eager, ambitious men. If such men come to the House, they are willing to leave it when opportunity offers. John J. Fitzgerald, of New York, after rising high on the Democratic side, and after long service, left of his own accord. James W. Good, Chairman of the Committee on Appropriations, has just done the same thing. Of course, any of them would leave to go to the Senate.

This aspect of Washington, this balance of profit and loss, was often in the thoughts of Henry Adams. He relates that he and John Hay and Clarence King often discussed the question: "Hay had a simple faculty for remembering faces, and would break off suddenly the thread of his talk, as he looked out of the window on Lafayette Square, to notice an old corps commander or admiral of the Civil War tottering along to his club for his cards or his cocktail...or what drew Adams's close attention: 'There goes old Boutwell gamboling like the gamboling kid.' There they went! Men who had swayed the course of empire as well as the course

of Hay, King, and Adams, less valued than the
ephemeral Congressman behind them, who could not
have told whether the general was a Boutwell or Boutwell a general. Theirs was the highest known success,
and one asked what it was worth to them. Apart
from personal vanity, what would they sell it for?"

Washington is full of ghosts ; the men who were.

The game of politics, like the game of chess, while
intricate and susceptible of many variations, is gov-
erned by fixed and ancient rules and conventions. A
Persian chess master having no language but his own,
and no contact or acquaintance or understanding or
even faint knowledge of the Western world, could yet
come to Washington, Georgia, and there in the shade
and repose and peace of that fine old town meet and
play the local expert in the perfect ease and security of
any meeting on a thoroughly known ground. With the
chessmen arranged between them, the players would
know without a spoken word or any other channel of
communication what to do next. They would be on
familiar ground. They would know the moves. They
would have a broad field of contact. The Georgia villager might soon find himself in closer mental com-
munion with the Persian than with any of his neighbors.

Politicians among us are set apart like that. Many
of them — a great many too many of them — follow
the game for a livelihood. They become professionals
in their engrossing vocation. Politics is the only game

that has no penalties of suspension or disbarment for fouls and unfair practices. There are no rules against gouging and biting and scratching and hitting below the belt. Men seek to rise to attain temporary aggrandizement and office, to overcome their opponents by any guile or subterfuge. In their old age they are embittered and their lives are ashes in their mouths. Their days of activity are spent in the vain pursuit of illusions and not in solid achievement. In the end they are "lame ducks" who must be "taken care of," or, if they fall out of the game inopportunely when their old cronies and associates are not in power, they go back where they came from and "resume the practice of law."

Their daily life is one of appalling transitions. One day it takes three or four messengers to conduct them in proper state from the entrance of their offices to their desks and relieve them of hat and coat. To see the great man appointments have to be made well in advance through a reluctant secretary, and the time of audience is restricted. It may be that the next time you see him, he will be hanging precariously on the rear platform of a street-car and, oh ! so eager to talk about anything and as long as you like. The heavy curse that hangs over the "ins" is that sooner or later they will be "outs," and the one hope that sustains the "outs," and prevents them from giving away to despair and going to work to earn a living, is that presently a turn of the wheel will bring them "in."

Being what they are, and permeated with the instinct for their guild, the politicians resent the intrusion of amateurs and persons with new ideas and new plans, or who do not know the old conventions. They hate anything new like the very devil. They cannot cope with it. They have no apparatus or formula to apply to new problems or new approaches. They like established and familiar issues. They like to deal with other professionals.

Too many good men and able have heeded Plutarch's advice. He said: Abstain from beans; that is, keep out of public offices, for anciently the choice of the officers of state was made by beans.

AIDE-ING THE PRESIDENT

SCENE: A West Point section-room. Time: 1927.

The first section in Social Science is discovered sitting on slim gilt chairs in a well-appointed room. A silver tea-service, the kettle hissing on the hob, and the tea-table, provided with cream-jug, sugar-bowl, and a small dish filled with thin slices of lemon, occupies an advantageous position near the softly burning cannel-coal fire. The room is cozy and well-lighted. The section is composed of youths handsome even according to the high West Point standard. They have learned how to sit on the fragile chairs without seeming apprehensive. They are of the *corps d'élite*, the Military Aides Division, undergoing special preparation for detail to the White House after graduation. The instructor is a woman who has qualified herself for the high and important work by several years' experience as a social secretary at Washington. A curate, holding plates containing thin slices of buttered bread and little cakes, stands beside the tea-table. The recitation begins.

Hostess-Instructor. "The young gentlemen who acted as visiting ladies will serve to-day those who performed the duties of aides at the last recitation."

Straightway there ensues a well-bred and well-ordered commotion. Half of the section remains seated and uncrosses its legs. The other half rises, and, murmuring, "One or two lumps, please?" and, "Shall I give you cream or a slice of lemon?" proceeds to cluster about the tea-table and execute the orders they have received. The Hostess-Instructor watches their every movement with a keen and critical eye and makes suggestions and comments. Finally, when the tea has been poured and distributed:

Hostess-Instructor. "Now, I hope you young gentlemen have thoroughly prepared your social-chatter lesson. Mr. Dash will recite first."

Cadet Dash arises from his chair and throwing himself into an attitude of unstudied grace, begins to murmur in a beautifully modulated voice a string of the polite nothings that pass muster as conversation around official tea-tables. After the other members of the section have each recited in turn, the Hostess-Instructor presents to them the following list of questions with the request that answers be returned at the next recitation:

"If the Speaker of the House of Representatives and the Chief Justice of the Supreme Court arrived at the same moment, which would be presented and served first?"

"In functions participated in by the President, the Vice-President, the Secretary of State, and ambassadors of foreign powers, state the order of precedence."

"At the President's New-Year reception, which is received first, the public printer, the Librarian of

Congress, or the president of the Columbian Institute for the Deaf and Dumb?"

"What system have you for memorizing which of the wives of Cabinet members and ambassadors take lemon and which cream in their tea, and how many lumps of sugar, if any?"

The members of the section take formal good-bye of the Hostess-Instructor, and after a profusion of bows retire from the room in their settled order of precedence.

Yes, indeed, Eunice, it looked at one time as if something like this might come to pass. Where the demand was so active it seemed incredible that the supply should not be created. The Military Aide at the White House reached his highest flower of beauty and usefulness in the Roosevelt and Taft administrations. He was very much a figure in those days. He fell into eclipse in the Wilson days after the President came in contact with the admirable and invaluable Admiral Grayson. Mr. Wilson was first busy and then at war and then ill and had no use for social butterflies. And that precisely is what a Military Aide is, an officer of the Quartermaster Corps, or the cavalry, or whatever arm of the service, detailed to the White House to make himself useful socially as the President or his wife may direct. It is a life full of odd and singular and trivial adventure. It is not clear yet what and how much use Mr. Harding will make of those who have been assigned to him. I have only seen them at garden parties and that was not a true test. The winter season is their great time.

To the present juncture the only military man President Harding has had about him is that freshly made one, his personal physician, Brigadier-General Charles E. Sawyer. And General Sawyer is not a social butterfly. Far be it from so. He is a genial little scout, full of droll stories, and can make a good after-dinner speech that will evoke roars of laughter even in these dry times, but over the teacups he would be a total loss and no insurance. In choosing his personal physician as his personal aide Mr. Harding is following Mr. Wilson's example, though never was a soldier turned out of more incurably civilian material than when the magic words were pronounced that made the Marion homœopath a brigadier. But presently Mrs. Harding may discover how useful can be some of the handsome lads of the army and navy who have been assigned to the White House. When she does, the Military Aide will perhaps come again into his old high and lofty estate.

I remember and can tell the first time I ever saw a military aide to the President earning his salary as fixed by law. It was at a reception at the White House when Mr. Roosevelt was President. In those days all persons invited to White House receptions were divided into two parts, just like Seidlitz powders, and provided with white and blue tickets of admission. I had a white ticket; so did several thousand other persons. We outnumbered the blue tickets more than ten to one; we were the popular branch. The blue tickets went in at the front door and met the President before the white tickets were admitted to his presence.

We went in at the east entrance of the White House opposite the Treasury Building, and left our coats and rubber shoes in little racks in the long corridor normally devoted to the glass cabinets containing plates used on the White House dinner-table when Millard Fillmore and Rutherford B. Hayes and Benjamin Harrison and others were President. Presently we trailed upstairs in a long queue across the central reception hall, through the family dining-room and the big state dining-room, through the Red Room, and into the presence of Mr. Roosevelt. As we shuffled nearer and nearer, we noted that opposite the President and Mrs. Roosevelt stood two military officers in full uniform. Gold belts were strapped about their waists and at their sides hung swords. They were introducing the long line to the President and his wife. One of them I knew. We had known each other for a long time. Yet when I came up to him he looked me straight in the eye and asked in a voice intended for my ear alone,

"What name, please?"

"McDermott," said I, in a clear, penetrating voice. As one who might announce, "We-have-with-us-to-night," the captain bowed to the President and presented in a loud, firm voice,

"Mr. President, Mr. Frelinghuysen."

The President grabbed my hand as though he had been waiting for me all the evening, as though all that had gone before was mere waste, and that for him, at least, the climax of the evening had come. "How-de-do, Mr. Willingham?" he said: "it is a real pleasure to see you here to-night." A confused memory of the bobbing heads of the wives of the Cabinet, and I found myself in the East Room. My experience had been that of a dry leaf caught in a strong draught.

Later in the evening I went up to my friend the captain.

"Why did you tell the President that my name was Frelinghuysen?" I asked him.

He looked at me in blank amazement.

"I didn't even know you were here," he said.

I told him what he had done. Then he confessed.

"To tell you the truth," he said, "after the first two or three hundred go by I can't distinguish one face from another. It's hard even to tell the men from the women. Everything gets sort of blurred before my eyes. It's hard to catch the names. People won't speak clearly. Besides, I had on a pair of new boots to-night and nothing else mattered much. Did you ever stand up in a pair of new boots from nine o'clock until a quarter of eleven asking people their names and then repeating them in a loud, clear voice?"

My next view of a military aide on active service was at a reception given by the Vice-President to the members of the Senate. It was the usual sort of thing. There was a sound of revelry by night, and mineral water flowed like champagne. The light, dry rattle of airy persiflage filled the air:

"Who's that dodo in the corner with the pink feathers in her hair?"

"My dear, he's had six glasses already, and there he is taking another. I declare he hasn't moved away from that table to-night."

"So good of you. Won't you come in on Thursday?"

"Yes, they always do things rather well here. I like to come."

"How hot the rooms are!"

"Let's slip upstairs and smoke a cigarette."

Suddenly the five members of the Marine Band, barricaded by potted palms at the head of the stairway, struck into "Hail to the Chief." Everybody knew what that meant. There was a pause, and then we heard a clanking sound as though some one was dragging a nest of coal-scuttles up the marble stairs. Presently there came in view the President and his wife, followed by two resplendent creatures in full uniforms, the scabbards of their swords banging against the steps as they mounted. It was an impressive entrance. We welcomed them to our midst.

But these two instances disclose only the smallest

part of the duties of an aide to the President. They must be ready and willing and able to do anything once. They are paid union wages, but they aren't allowed to keep or to have an eight-hour day. Two soldiers ideally qualified and fitted to become military aides at the White House were old Abdullah Bulbul Ameer and Ivan Petroski Skivar. Their glory is preserved in deathless song:

> The sons of the Prophet are hardy and grim
>   And quite unaccustomed to fear,
> But most reckless by far both of life and of limb
>   Was Abdullah Bulbul Ameer.
>
> If you wanted a man to encourage the van
>   Or to harass the foe in the rear,
> Or to storm a redoubt, you had only to shout
>   For Abdullah Bulbul Ameer.
>
> There are brave men in plenty and well known to fame
>   In the army that fights for the Tsar,
> But bravest by far was a man by the name
>   Of Ivan Petroski Skivar.
>
> He could imitate Irving, tell fortunes at cards,
>   Or play on the Spanish guitar;
> In fact, quite la crême de la crême of the Guards
>   Was Ivan Petroski Skivar.

To be able to imitate Irving, tell fortunes with cards, and play on the Spanish guitar — that gives some idea of the range, the versatility, the adaptability that should be possessed by an aide to the President. When President Taft was making one of his trips around the country, an editor down South, who had watched the doings in his town, went back to his office and wrote this editorial paragraph:

"President Taft is having the time of Archie Butt's life."

Captain Archie Butt was President Taft's chief and favorite aide. He could do anything that old Abdullah Bulbul Ameer or Ivan Petroski Skivar could do, and then wouldn't be half started. He walked, rode, played golf, went shopping, played bridge, attended baseball games, and traveled with the President. He attended concerts, theaters, went shopping with and helped Mrs. Taft at her teas. He dined and lunched at the White House almost every time the President gave a party. He helped make up the invitation lists for the state receptions and dinners, and knew how to fix the gramophone when it got out of order. He was about the best-liked and most popular man in Washington.

Mr. Roosevelt began the practice of having military aides in attendance on his person when he went abroad on formal occasions, but he did not take one with him every time he stirred about nor did he make them invariably wear their uniforms. It remained for Mr. Taft to develop the possibilities of the military aide as a companion and as an object to delight the eye of the civilian beholder. Mr. Roosevelt used to ride in Rock Creek Park, and practice his horse over some low jumps that had been erected for his use. He used to pick his military aides from young men in the army who had famous names: Lee, Grant, Sheridan, Henry, and the like. Young Fitzhugh Lee was for a long time his favorite riding companion.

The aides are much courted socially. It is popularly supposed to lie in their power to do much for persons who entertain social designs upon the White House. They are greatly besought for favors. They are very discreet and are never tempted to let become public the contents of some of the amusing and surprising requests they receive from persons who desire to be favored above others invited to the White House.

HAYS: A HUMAN FLIVVER

WILL HAYS doesn't belong to the Post-Office Department. He ought to be out at the Bureau of Standards in the case in the vault with the meter bar and the kilogram from which all our standards of weights and measures are derived. For Mr. Hays is a standard of measure and of value himself. He is the one hundred per cent American we have all heard so much talk about. Submit him to any test and you get a perfect reaction. He doesn't even stain the litmus paper. Apply any native or domestic standard and he complies with it to a hair-line. He is as indigenous as sassafras root. He is one of us. He is folks. As such I like him and as such I sing him.

I have noted a lamentable disposition in certain quarters to speak lightly of Mr. Hays. This must stop. When we make light of him, we make light of and decry our peculiar national institutions, our native civilization. He is a human flivver, the most characteristic native product; a two-cylinder single-seater, good for more miles per gallon than any other make of man. He takes you there and brings you back, in the blessed phrase, thus satisfying a great national ideal. He is as much a national institution and as purely native as the practice of buying enlarged crayon portraits or talking machines on the installment plan.

Mr. Hays cannot be described or interpreted or

treated in terms of the eminent Cato style of thing. That is not his line at all. Besides, as everybody knows, Cato was a foreigner as well as a sourball. On both counts it is a case of thumbs down for him.

Unhappily for the truth and for our present understanding of the public men about us, there has lingered through the ages a superstition that we must cling to the old classic models in observing and commenting upon statesmen and holders of high office. Under this outworn practice we must think of them as wearing togas and speaking in rotund, sonorous phrases from which one in schoolboy days sought out through many weary hours the gerund and the gerundive or what not, as the masters ordered. Whereas, if you pick up a *Congressional Record*, you find them actually saying:

"The two Prussianizing influences working like comajenes to undermine the army are the classification system and the General Staff, headed by Sir John Pershing, whose ideals and methods are utterly at variance with the best traditions of America. Under these two institutions injustices sprung up during the war and are still bearing fruit. It is not service nor merit that count. Favoritism, pull, intrigue, standing in with the man above, all play a more important part than record, ability, and understanding of and power to handle men. Preference is given to men who spend their energy in flattering their superiors instead of defeating the enemy. . . ."

No, you cannot make much of Mr. Hays by apply-

SECRETARY HUGHES AND POSTMASTER-GENERAL HAYS

ing the classic standards. He derives more nearly from Mr. Addison Sims of Seattle than he does from Cato. If some alchemist in biology (if you know what I mean) could extract the essential juices from Mr. Addison Sims and all the typical Rotarians, he might produce a sort of pale, synthetic Will Hays, but there still would be qualities missing. For he is an articulate emotionalist if ever there was one; a politician to his finger-tips and a strong josher; a real handshaker and elbow massager. He is the English sparrow of the Harding administration: chipper, confident, unafraid, friendly. And he behaves as such.

You must have read a paragraph, as I did, in the newspapers not long ago telling how Postmaster-General Hays has hung his office latchstring out in fact. The word "private" has vanished from the door and you just walk in when you want to see him. Inside you'll find a huge room with Mr. Hays at his desk in one corner and a lot of chairs scattered around. Mr. Hays will hand you his engagement list for the day and you can see for yourself how he is fixed for time, pick out your own slice of any not already appropriated, and then camp in a chair across the room until your time comes. Conferences are held in sight if not in actual hearing of everybody who happens to be in the room, and there is no usher, no secretary, confidential clerk, messenger, or other functionary to deal with.

This procedure does not apply to Senators; but,

then, no rule or procedure does apply to them in Washington.

You must have read also how Mr. Hays dictates to three stenographers at once and how he arrived at his office one day before any of the clerks had reported. Well, it's all true. I thought it was press-agent stuff, and the most perfunctory and conventional press-agent stuff at that, until I went down to the Post-Office Department to find out for myself. But the performance is actually put on as advertised. Any one may come in. Seats free, strangers welcome.

I was glad I was curious enough to go, for I encountered a Greek valet that Mr. Hays has inherited or acquired from Colonel George Harvey. This boy — he is a mere lad — is seeing life. During the war he was an interpreter with the British forces in Mesopotamia. After the war he came to New York and got a job as a waiter in the Knickerbocker Hotel. When the Knickerbocker went out of business, Mr. Regan, the proprietor, passed the youth on to his friend, Colonel Harvey, as a valet of sorts. When the new ambassador went to London, the Greek was left behind with Will Hays. But not as a valet. Never! Never! The most trustworthy and detailed accounts of American history fail to reveal a single instance where a man in or from Sullivan County, Indiana, ever needed or employed a valet to help him put on his clothes or take care of his wardrobe.

"I want to *pro*-gress," said the Greek.

"I want him to be useful," said Will Hays, and at once started him to learning typewriting on a second-hand machine.

And now, as the heir of all the ages sits on the eighth floor of the Post-Office Building, pegging away at "Now is the time for all good men to come to the aid of the party," and contemplating his new boss, I would give a hat to know his unvarnished, actual impression of him. I may add that the Greek is not on the Government pay-roll. He is a private venture in Americanization which is being conducted under the personal supervision and at the private expense of the Postmaster-General.

Mr. Hays is at least a contemporary, if not a modernist. He believes in the form of Government of the United States, the Presbyterian Church of which he is an elder, as was his father before him, and the Republican Party. He accepts and concedes the advantage of such modern things as stem-winding watches, self-starters, and demountable rims. He is not hidebound. And if I may venture to introduce our native speech into these undefiled precincts, I'll tell the world that he wears snappy clothes. Not all the young men in all the spring clothing advertisements have anything on him as a nobby dresser.

He honestly believes, too, in the freedom of the press, and does not fear that Max Eastman or anybody else can make a dent, much less impede, retard, or impair, the institutions and principles he cherishes.

The day that I called upon him to verify his open-door policy he was considering the case of the *Liberator*, and we talked about it.

Mr. Hays was clearly puzzled to discover a reason or rule of action that made a publication unfit to associate in the mails with other second-class matter, but mailable at a higher rate of postage. It was no surprise when he restored the *Liberator* to the second-class privilege and refunded the excess postage that had been paid. Also I came away with the impression that Mr. Hays has not forgotten what he learned in his schoolboy days, that gas, hot air, or steam commonly are not dangerous or destructive unless confined and compressed. Given a vent they are just vapors (or vaporings) and will do no harm. Mr. Hays very plainly does not want to be a censor; he is sure about that.

Mr. Hays couldn't be other than what he is — a typical native product, for he comes from what Joe Mitchell Chapple would call the great throbbing heart of the country, meaning Sullivan, Sullivan County, Indiana, which is right on the edge of the center of population. He is not a rustic. But neither is he urban. Certainly he is not suburban, as I once thought. Groping for the right phrase, I should say he is more like a visiting Elk who knows his way about. He is forty years old. He has been in politics all his life. He is interested and engrossed in the game every day in the year. He was a precinct committeeman before he was twenty-one. Being a Republican chairman of something or other has been his life career. He has been chairman of his county committee, State Advisory Committee, speakers' bureau of the State Committee, district chairman, and chairman of the State Central Committee, and finally chairman of the Republican National Committee. He has come to the end of the chairmanships his party has to offer. He has played out the string.

One of his ideas, he told me, is that everybody should get into politics. He wants more politics rather than less politics. His great aspiration is to get all the war workers, all the dollar-a-year men, all the Liberty Loan drive men and women, all the Red Cross volunteers, all the canteen workers, to transfer the energies they put into war activities into politics. Hays expressed this belief to me one day:

"The day is passing when men will tolerate anywhere in this country any practices in politics that they would not commend in the strictest business and professional affairs. When we get our politics entirely on this basis, when we live our patriotism daily, we will do a citizen's full duty, and not until then. I repeat, I have no use for the individual who is either 'too busy' or 'too good' to help. He has no just complaint to make, whatever happens. He is riding on another's ticket. I have an abiding faith that there will be an awakened sense of civic duty as one of the by-products of the war.

"I repeat, and shall continually declare, that what we need in this country is not 'less politics,' but more attention to politics. Politics is the science of government, and what we need is more attention to the science of government. We fought in France to make certain everywhere that men should have the right to govern themselves, and here in this country, where we have that privilege, I insist that we exercise it."

While I have not read every page of it, I know that his life is an open book, for he has been in nearly every big factional fight in Indiana for twenty years, and I have known fights out there so bitter and so searching that they were willing to go back to a man's great-great-grandfather, and what he had done to the Indians, to get something on him. Hays has come through as clean as a smelt. He is a shrewd, lively, industrious, average human being, having a very good time out of life. He is not a great man, but, then, who is here at Washington — or anywhere else? Mostly they seem to be running in the medium sizes these days.

Mr. Hays is doing a good job in the Post-Office Department. He is restoring its morale and its efficiency by great leaps. A few days after he was sworn in he met, was introduced to, and spoke to all of the two thousand Post-Office Department employees in Washington. Even "Old Tom," the Post-Office cat, was greeted. Then he went to the New York and Chicago post-offices and met and spoke to all the employees there. He was putting what he calls "heart" into them. The procedure has been an immense success. To all of them Mr. Hays said:

"Every effort shall be exercised to humanize the department. Labor is not a commodity. That idea was abandoned nineteen hundred and twenty-one years ago next Easter. In this department are three hundred thousand employees. They have the brain and they have the hand to do the job well; and they shall have the heart to do it well. We purpose to approach this matter so that they shall be partners with us in this business. It is a great human institution touching every individual in the country. It is a great business institution serving every individual in the country. I know that with three hundred thousand men and women pledged to serve all the people and honestly discharging that duty, fairly treated, and properly appreciated, all partners with us here in this great enterprise, we can do the job. It's going to be done."

That, he has found, is the stuff to give the troops. It bucks 'em up, and now they all swear by him and believe in him. And so, as he dashes about arriving at Cabinet meetings a little breathlessly and always with not more than five seconds to spare before the President enters the cabinet room, he seems fairly content, for he is taking his hills on high. And that is always a satisfaction.

WOOD: OUR LONE PRO-CONSUL

It would have been too absurd if we could have done no better for Leonard Wood than to give him as the capstone of his varied career the Provostship of the University of Pennsylvania. Not that it isn't an honorable post of high distinction, but it is so entirely out of General Wood's line of country. He is not an educator. He is our lone pro-consul. Under our peculiar form of government, as devised by what President Harding will call the "founding fathers," there is no career for a pro-consul and colonial administrator.

General Wood would have done much better to have been born in England. Then he wouldn't have had to cast about as he has in recent years for an outlet for his energies, his wholesome ambition, and his desire for effective public service. When the Government which General Wood organized in Cuba ran down and stopped ticking in 1906 because the Cubans did not keep it wound up, Mr. Roosevelt sent a one-time Nebraska lawyer down there to be Governor-General. It is an incurably casual way we have.

For more than twenty years General Wood applied himself to mastering the profession of arms. He became our best-known professional soldier at home and abroad. Not only best-known, but I am willing to concede our best-equipped officer. Certainly he is so rated by the keenest professional opinion in England

SECRETARY WEEKS AND GENERAL WOOD

and on the continent of Europe. Then the war came along and the President as Commander-in-Chief, acting within his discretion under the statutes made and provided in such cases (General Pershing eagerly assenting), kept General Wood out of the war. That, of course, was a heavy cross for him to bear. He had a right to feel frustrated. He didn't complain. A good many people shared General Wood's feelings. There was a fairly widespread public sense that something ought to be done about it. So the General became a candidate for the Republican nomination for the presidency. That was a curious adventure.

Julius Cæsar and George Washington and Oliver Cromwell and Ulysses S. Grant and Andrew Jackson and Theodore Roosevelt and quite a number of others managed successfully to combine the professions of arms, statesmanship, politics, and office-holding, but General Wood couldn't quite bring it off. Times have changed, and for the moment, at least, there is a sound public instinct among us against placing military personages in high civil office.

To Major-General Wood, running for the presidency was an open process openly arrived at. His was not a bashful candidacy. He was unlike any presidential candidate I ever saw ; and I have been much exposed to them. He was difficult to focus either as a soldier among politicians or as a politician whose true function is soldiering. It was easy to decide that he was a better soldier than he was a politician, for he is no politician at all. He long had a hankering for politics, but every time he dipped into that turbid pool he imperiled his status as a soldier. I suspect he was not alert enough. It is enough that the politicians thought of him as a soldier and many soldiers regarded him enviously as a politician and attributed his eminence to his political qualities and acumen. Certainly he was not a typical politician. He was not a typical army officer, either, for he had and has a sound knowledge of the great world and its affairs.

Nor can I give him my vote in any public award of the Roosevelt mantle. Roosevelt was an eager, ardent, practicing politician and public man who liked to think of himself as a soldier, which, of course, he was not, for he had no sense of subordination or discipline. He enjoyed to the utmost the brief adventure of the Spanish War, but he never would or could have endured the rigidity and monotony and effacement of army routine. General Wood, on the other hand, as I see him, is an army man who likes to think of himself as a statesman and public man. He has a perfect right to think of himself in that capacity, too, and have his dreams. But he has got to show qualities and attributes not yet revealed before his dreams come true.

He is a solid man. The upper part of his body is finely developed. His arms, wrists, and hands are large and thick and powerful. His legs seem too short and thin for the immense torso and barrel they have to carry. This impression is accentuated by his lameness, for his left leg drags perceptibly when he walks.

Though he is sixty years old, his head is well thatched with blond hair; no indication of baldness anywhere. He has kept his hair. His face is impassive and rather heavy in repose. It doesn't light up much even when he talks about the things that interest him. Indeed, he is as undemonstrative a person as you will encounter in a day's walk. His emotions (if any, as the income-tax forms say) lie deep and are well under control. He may be a charter member of the "strong, silent man" group, but I do not get that impression. It may be that his apperceptions and antennæ are not as sensitive as some other persons'. He is not quick to take fire. He is not colorful; he does not glow. At any rate, he did not glow for me, though I blew and blew trying to kindle a flame.

General Wood has a distinct charm of manner as a social being, and I understand perfectly why people who are associated with him like him and swear by him. His voice is low, pleasant, agreeable, and well modulated. He speaks without gesture and without emphasis or marked inflection. Even when he is making a speech he does not gesticulate, but stands in one posture, with his right hand grasping his left wrist behind him. He is an effective speaker in a simple, direct fashion, without heat or passion or rising to the heights, and a really interesting talker.

He was in uniform when last I talked with him, and

one that showed traces of his brief service abroad as a military observer during the war. Instead of two tin stars on his shoulders, his insignia of rank was embroidered, after the French fashion, in silver gilt, and he wore cord breeches lighter in color than his khaki tunic.

Also I was amused to note how he had taken the Sam out of the Sam Browne belt and thus brought himself within regulations. He was girt about the middle with a broad heavy belt, but had left off the distinguishing cross strap that lies diagonally across the chest over the right shoulder. This is a fashion set by Field Marshal Haig which many of our overseas officers followed.

Any one who comes in contact with General Wood must like his personality. He is a man of ability in his chosen field, but unfortunately for him or for us, that chosen field is not greatly cultivated here. Administering the affairs of an inferior or subject people through an army of occupation is one problem ; and that General Wood knows from experience. Administering the affairs of a free and noisy people, all hailing from Missouri, is something else again. Ask Mr. Taft or Mr. Wilson. Ask anybody. But General Wood was wholly within his rights in asking us to allow him to make the experiment. And the politicians who controlled the Chicago Convention of 1920 were equally wholly within their rights in declining the General's urgently made proffer and selecting Mr. Harding. It was just another one of those well-meant things that didn't come off.

I imagine the routine of the army looked bleak and dreary to General Wood after this high and engrossing emprise. He could not look for a high and active place. The Pershing faction had come into control, and that meant friction or effacement for Wood. Mr. Harding saved the situation when he offered to send him out to Manila as Governor-General, but even that post does not offer a very enthralling prospect to a man of sixty. Besides, he long ago went through that phase. He has done his full share of "pacifying" in our Eastern archipelago. He pacified the Moros. Once is enough of that sort of thing. The freshness is all worn off the Philippines as a scene of active adventure and enterprise. I, for one, do not wonder that General Wood turned a heeding ear to the University of Pennsylvania when it offered to make him Provost before the chance came to go again to the Philippines. It was something new, at any rate.

But what an unexpected road he has followed to bring him where he is. When he graduated from the Harvard Medical School his first services were given to the poor of Boston. Soon he became a contract surgeon in the army. That was the old name for a doctor hired by the army from civil life. He served through an Indian campaign in the Southwest and won the Congressional Medal of Honor. That is the highest military distinction we bestow. Then he got his chance. One apparently sure road to advancement in this broad expanse is becoming physician to a President. Dr. Wood was set on that highway.

When Grover Cleveland was President of the United States, he asked Daniel Lamont to secure for attendance at the White House the services of a suitable surgeon of the army. An officer, now a Major-General of the United States Army, was appealed to, and suggested Dr. Leonard Wood. After Mr. Cleveland left the White House, Dr. Wood continued as the attending physician to President McKinley. When the Spanish War broke out, McKinley commissioned him as the Colonel of the Rough Riders. Within a month after the first action against the enemy Wood was made a Brigadier-General of volunteers by President McKinley, and soon afterwards was placed in command of the troops and in charge of the civil administration of the Department of Santiago.

The military duties of General Wood at this time were insignificant in comparison with those of the civil administration. He cleaned the city, purged it of all tropical diseases, and turned it from a pest-hole into a modern city in which public works were installed. Roads and bridges were constructed, public buildings renovated or rebuilt, a school system was established, and the laws were executed.

At the end of a year Wood was made Governor-General of Cuba with instructions to convert Cuba into a self-sustaining republic. This work required the adoption of a new constitution, the rewriting of the laws of the island, the revision of public works, the installation of public schools, and in general all the machinery for the proper operation of any Government.

When the new State of Cuba was established as one of the independent republics of the world, Wood was sent by President Roosevelt to the Philippine Islands where he pacified Mindanao Province.

Richard Olney, at one time Secretary of State under Grover Cleveland, wrote : " . . . to congratulate you personally on the most successful and deservedly successful career, whether soldier or public man of any sort, that the Spanish War and its consequences have brought to the front."

At the end of his work in the Philippine Islands, Leonard Wood was called to Washington and made Chief of Staff of the army, where he undertook the preparatory work which later resulted in the student officers' camps and the business men's camps that ultimately produced, at the time of the declaration of war with Germany, approximately 40,000 partially trained officers who were made available for service with the new army to be raised and sent overseas.

At the end of his period as Chief of Staff, Leonard Wood was assigned to command the Department of the East. He then had the opportunity to put into active operation the Plattsburg Camps, and afterwards other students' camps throughout the country.

I think it entirely possible that General Wood's career is better known and more highly esteemed abroad than it is in this country. Here he has been and is an eminent but more or less unrelated figure. We have no niche, or place in our national filing system for pro-consuls or colonial administrators. As they say in business, we aren't organized to handle that class of goods. I think, too, we have a general feeling that we can pick up one when the need comes. That is General Wood's hard luck, and maybe our misfortune, but, anyhow, that is how we found him; just by chance. There may be another, if we ever need him.

THE GREAT HITCHCOCK ENIGMA

IF I was a young man in college studying politics, meaning, as that would mean, of course, the politics of Plato and Aristotle, I would add a touch of actuality to the proceeding by writing a thesis for a doctorate with this leading caption : "Does He Blow Out the Gas? — Being an Inquiry into the Habits and Activities of Frank H. Hitchcock Between Campaigns." I should not expect an undergraduate and an amateur to chart Mr. Hitchcock's activities while actually engaged in a campaign. Even the professionals can't always do that.

Mr. Hitchcock is a piece-work Warwick. He has a closed shop ; he doesn't admit apprentices, nor does he belong to the professional politicians' union. He is a specialist. His lay is picking Presidential candidates. This is not only a piece-work job, but essentially a seasonal occupation. Though Mr. Hitchcock has followed his precarious trade for many years — about fifteen, in fact — he is still free from any vocational stigmata. He is inscrutable, imperturbable, impenetrable, and notably close-mouthed. He offers no more inviting avenue of approach for scrutiny and communication than a well-made billiard ball. Not that he isn't civil, for he is ; but that, like Lord Tennyson's lady friend, he is icily regular, splendidly null. One never seems to get on, to get anywhere, no matter how prolonged the contact.

I know it is a horrid, vulgar little detail, but Mr. Hitchcock never sweats. Even at national conventions where, after two or three days, everybody wilts and begins to have the bedraggled aspect of something the cat has brought in, Mr. Hitchcock is as immaculate, as aloof, as specklessly arrayed as one of the superior young men in the collar advertisements. He might have just come out of the hands of a vacuum cleaner. Always he is like that. He greets the embarrassed gods nor fears to shake the iron hand of Fate or match with Destiny for beers — that sort of thing, if you know what I mean. John Oakhurst plus the young Talleyrand, plus a second carbon copy of the Admirable Crichton, plus the house of Kuppenheimer — that is the general impression.

And nobody seems to know what is his little game. Apparently it is not money. He seems just to like to back his fancy. He doesn't run in herds with, or as do, the other politicians. He plays a lone hand. He is always a figure apart. To me he is one of the most provocative, puzzling, and intriguing figures in the great intricate game of national politics. He provokes curiosity and inquiry.

Of this I am sure. He is a bred gamester with a cold passion for the hazard of high stakes and the rigor of keen play. He likes the matching of wits and the tortuous intrigues of politics. He plays at politics as other men play at poker or dice. Politics and "big business" are the only really big games that we support in this country. They are full of thrills for the men who play them.

In all his political career Mr. Hitchcock has never been attached to a cause or championed a principle. He has attached himself to men, or more precisely a man, and played with other men as pawns. We have always had such men in this adventurous, chance-loving country, but I do not recall one in politics quite so cool, so detached, so completely the technician and nothing else as Mr. Hitchcock. We have come to know fairly intimately and familiarly the private and personal side of most of the men who figure in national politics, or, at least, we like to think we have. The first natural inquiry we make about any man is, "What is his business?" "How did he make his money?" "How much has he got?" "What does he do for a living?" We always want to know that, don't we? It may be none of our business, but we ask the questions just the same — and usually, before we are done, get an answer.

Usually politicians find it to their interest to keep on public view all the time. No more than actors do they want to be forgotten. Frank Hitchcock and Maude Adams are the two exceptions to this rule. Mr. Hitchcock plays his brief quadrennial season, keeps out of the limelight while he is on the stage, and then disappears without trace. What is known about him?

I can quickly set down the meager data I have for an estimate. He was graduated from Harvard with the class of 1891. His first public job, I think, was as a timekeeper on the construction of the gray stone pile on Pennsylvania Avenue, that is the Post Office Department Building at Washington. Then he was a clerk in the Department of Agriculture. John G. Capers told me one night at a public dinner, when Hitchcock was there, that the then rising young man "used to sort bird feathers over at the Department of Agriculture." But that was only a bitter pleasantry. Capers and Hitchcock were not on good terms at the time, because of some difference over Republican politics in South Carolina.

However, Mr. Hitchcock is an amateur ornithologist of some repute, and a genuine bird-lover with a respectable knowledge of bird-lore. That was one of his points of contact with Theodore Roosevelt. This love of birds is his one revealing quality that I know about.

When I first knew Mr. Hitchcock he had left the Department of Agriculture and had come over to be chief clerk under Secretary Cortelyou of the then newly created Department of Commerce and Labor. He became a protégé and, in a sense, a disciple of Mr. Cortelyou, and followed in his footsteps. It was an understandable association. Any machine erected or constructed by either of these men ran on ball bearings and rubber tires. It never clanked. Clanking was a fault that neither of them could endure.

It was Mr. Cortelyou who put Mr. Hitchcock in

politics. Cortelyou went on from the Department of Commerce and Labor to manage Roosevelt's campaign, and became Postmaster-General. Four years later Hitchcock managed Taft's campaign and became, in turn, Postmaster-General. Since then he has been on his own.

Every fourth year that can be evenly divided by two — that is, every Presidential campaign year — brief, fugitive dispatches under Southern date-lines begin to appear in the newspapers. They say in substance: Mr. Hitchcock was here yesterday conferring with local Republican politicians. He declined to be interviewed or to discuss the purpose of his visit. The gossips and politicians at Washington read these, and begin to say: "Hitchcock is rounding up the Southern delegates." He is reputed to be a master hand with them.

I have heard many vague stories of how the twigs are limed for Southern delegates to Republican national conventions; how these wary, shy, sophisticated birds are captured and held together until the people's choice is ratified, but never until 1920 did I come upon a definite narrative by an actual participant.

The usual elusive fragmentary news came up from the South that year in the late winter and early spring. First it was rumored that Mr. Hitchcock was "for Lowden," but this was denied. The next surmise had him working for Wood, and when the fact did not materialize, Washington said in its expressive way.

"Hitchcock has not lighted." He did not light until late, for it was mid-March before he became associated with the Wood campaign. This was after John T. King had been eliminated and after Colonel William Cooper Procter's methods of management had proved not so subtle and deft as the situation seemed to require. As they said at the time, all the ivory did not go into the soap.

Along in May the Senate decided to inquire into the pre-convention campaign expenses of the Presidential candidates, and Mr. Hitchcock was the very first witness called. Let me isolate here a part of the story he told. The Senate didn't get much out of Mr. Hitchcock. I quote pertinent bits:

"I came to them [the Wood people] under the condition, when I entered the campaign, that I should not be called upon to collect campaign funds, and I have followed that policy. After the announcement of my connection with the campaign, various people from time to time sent in checks to me, and I turned them over to the organization. The total of these checks did not exceed from $20,000 to $25,000 for the entire campaign.

"My function has been largely advisory, supervisory. I have endeavored to interest the political leaders of the country that I knew, friends of mine and men that I have known in previous campaigns, in the Wood cause. That has been my principal work."

"Suppose it was decided to set up contesting delegations [in the South], would that question be referred to you?"

"I have never set up any contesting delegations, and never intend to. I do not believe in that sort of thing.

"The principal contest that has developed since I have been in the movement is the contest in Georgia, and the organization in Georgia is headed by the State Chairman, who is recognized by the National Committee, and with the approval of the National Committeeman, recognized by our National Committee. That organization is being contested."

"How much money have you sent there?"

"I think a total from the Washington and New York headquarters of $10,000. At first $5000 was sent, and then it was reported to us that the opposition in the State was flooding the State with money, and they asked for additional funds, and we sent $5000 additional."

"What salaries do the Wood headquarters pay?"

"I do not know a single salary. I do not get any, naturally. I furnish my own room, and I have received no money whatever from the Wood organization for any purpose."

Well, there you are. I might go on and give details of the trafficking as they were related by other witnesses, but that would be aside from my present point. Mr. Hitchcock did not figure in the squalid details. He was not there.

What else he is interested in besides politics I don't

know. Like a far-off planetary body sweeping along its solitary orbit, he is discernible for a brief period every fourth year in the umbra or penumbra of some Presidential candidate. If he picks a dead one, as, poor dear, he so frequently does, he goes out like a candle about the middle of June. In the last Presidential campaign he made a momentary reappearance in July. I heard of him sitting on the front row when Harding was notified of his nomination at Marion. And even while we look he fades away into the void, softly, softly, softly.

What happens to him? Where does he go? There is your problem and your mystery.

NORRIS: A NATIVE PRODUCT

HOMESPUN is the best wear. The important thing about common people is that there are so many of them and, like common things, they are so necessary. They bear all the burdens. All over the world this is the day of common men. All values are reckoned in averages. An English observer, my friend Philip Gibbs, recently among us, has noted rightly enough:

"It is a nation of nobodies, great with the power of the common man and the plain sense that governs his way of life. Other nations are still ruled by their 'somebodies' — by their pomposities and high panjandrums. But it is the nobodies whose turn is coming in history, and America is on their side."

By "nobodies" Gibbs means, of course, the average run of mankind. He has phrased it badly, for among us, certainly, the "nobodies," as he calls them, are in the aggregate the Great Somebody. I am not skilled enough in the terminology of "classes" to know where the proletariat ends and the bourgeoisie begins. I do not take any stock in the present-day effort to divide us into layers or strata with class distinctions. My hero is the average man.

With this brief prelude I present to you George William Norris, the junior Senator from Nebraska. I submit and proclaim that Norris is the Average American, and as such I celebrate him. If you want to know

America, you must know Norris first. Not only is he the Average American, but he is the average of all the average home-bred citizens of the Republic. He is the least common multiple, the lowest common denominator, the greatest common divisor.

What Norris thinks, what Norris believes, is what, in the long run, a clear majority of the country thinks and believes. He is not an extraordinary person. If you think that, you miss the point. He is the supreme, perfect type of the ordinary person, and a most useful man to know and watch in this time of social and economic flux and change and bewilderment and upheaval. If you do not know him, I am doing you a favor to introduce you to him. In a large way of speaking, nothing that vitally affects all of us can come to pass in this country unless the Norris type approves of it. He is the symbol of the forces which make final decisions with us.

Get on any train in the corn and hog States anywhere between Chicago and Lincoln, Nebraska, and you will find a dozen men like George William Norris. They are earnest folk, probably have a Sunday-School class at home, and smoke five-cent cigars with a relish which is the truest and surest visible manifestation among adult males of real leaders of the simple life. They have a first-hand grasp of the simple elements of public affairs and a rough-working knowledge of national governmental machinery and procedure. They do not know the subtleties and chicanery and the

SENATOR GEORGE W. NORRIS

wheels within wheels of politics as it is played in the East.

There aren't many men like Norris in the large Eastern cities, at least not in politics. But in the Middle West they are becoming, if they are not already, the dominant type. They are plain, simple people who have worked hard all their lives and who have known what it is to be poor, but not the squalid, sordid poverty of the congested East that kills hope and crushes the life and strength and self-respect out of men. I should say that the strongest characteristic of men of the Norris type (it seems impossible to differentiate him in any way from the type) is a strong and active feeling of fellowship. They are marked by a notable desire to be helpful to those who have not been so fortunate. As nearly as possible they want every one to share and share alike the common privileges of human society. They are good, useful citizens — not "prominent citizens," but useful citizens. There is a whole world of difference.

If George Norris ever declares for the proletariat revolution, I, for one, will begin to make ready for its coming. Norris is the surest political barometer in the United States. He can't help being it. It is an inherent quality, like the wetness of water. He is on the dominant and majority side in any great mass movement in this country under the operation of a natural law that is just as sure and irresistible and inevitable as the law which compels water to seek its own level.

Mr. Wilson could not get the country in a mind to go to war until Norris and his like were clearly satisfied that it was the right thing to do. When they saw the righteousness of it, the rest was easy. I believe you could have found nowhere any clearer vision and understanding of the processes of mind of the country at large, while public opinion was making on the league of nations and the peace treaty, than by observing Norris's mental reactions as he changed from an ardent believer in the league idea to one of the "bitter-ender" opponents of the league and treaty. Take his own words:

"I started this thing in good faith. No man had more honest and beautiful intentions than I had when that peace conference met at Versailles. No man in all the world was more anxious to have a permanent peace than I. No man under any flag would sacrifice more, according to what he had to sacrifice, than I would to have brought about a league that was honest and honorable. I believed that our allies were honest and honorable. I thought they were square; I thought they were fair; and when the league of nations part of the treaty was first given to the world, while I disliked some of it very much, I was almost on the point of swallowing it. I was willing to sacrifice almost anything to get the right kind of league of nations. To me it seemed that Article X was almost damnable. I thought that the article providing for disarmament might not mean anything, and other things the same way; and yet I said to myself, 'They are honest, we are honest, and if all of us are going into this honestly, I can overlook a good many things that don't seem right.'

"Later it developed what they had done in making the treaty; but although it seemed to me there were a lot of sins even in the league as they had promulgated it, when the treaty came forth it made the league look like a banner of purity compared to the deceit, the wrong, and the sin that was bound up in that treaty.

"When I discovered that these same men who had talked eloquently here to us had in their pockets secret treaties when they did it; when I discovered that they pulled out those secret treaties at the peace table, in contravention and in contradiction to every agreement that they made when we entered the peace conference; when I saw that they were demanding that these secret treaties be legalized; and, more than all, when I saw our own President lie down and give in and submit to the disgrace, the dishonor, the crime, and the sin of that treaty, then I said: 'Great God! I don't believe I want to have any dealings with any of you people. I am suspicious of you all the way through. You are dishonest. You have not been fair with us or with the world. You have been wicked. You have concluded to act here just the same as you were acting in barbarous days, after proclaiming to us and after we believed that you were in earnest and fighting for democracy to build a peace, a world peace, a league of nations that would bring peace and happiness forever to a suffering people.'

"I think any honest believer in the religion of Jesus Christ, when he understands what we are asked to do, would suffer death before he would advise us to give our official sanction to the treaty as it stands."

Now the sole interest and value of Norris's state of mind and of his fervent declaration about the sin inherent in the treaty is that he believes it to his depths and that he would go to the stake for his conviction. The seat of popular opinion and political control in the United States resides and has resided for some years in that vast stretch of fertile territory between the Alleghanies and the intermountain States of the West. It is the Mississippi Valley and the States on either side of it. That is the heart of this country; that is the producing area; that is where the corn and the hogs and the wheat and the ore and the oil and the cotton and the sugar come from. We are what we are as a people because they are what they are. Roughly speaking, the rest of us outside of that land of fatness derive our sustenance and existence by trafficking in and fabricating what they produce. Now Norris is of the very pith and marrow and sinew of these people. He thinks as they think, he lives as they live, his processes of thought are their processes of thought.

Norris is of average size, well-muscled and wiry. He is quiet in manner, with an open, frank, friendly face. His rough hair is gray. He is as industrious as a beaver. When one comes to describe him, one sees that there isn't an extraordinary thing about him. He is the average American born of clean stock in a farming country who has lived all his life upon a plane of perfect equality and upon terms of absolute democracy with his neighbors. That was one of the interesting things about the "insurgency" movement which brought Norris to the fore in the House and eventually in the Senate. Its propulsive force and motive power came from average men. It was an average man's movement. It is doubly interesting now as a social phenomenon, as foreshadowing the present world-wide groping among common average men for a more equitable diffusion of authority and responsibility in self-government.

For a taste of the simple quality of the man take this confession of faith made the other day on the Senate floor. Norris had talked for three days about the oppression of the Koreans and Chinese by the Japanese. He had urged that the Japanese were trying with all their might to stamp out Christianity in the Orient. Then this autobiographical revelation:

"I am not a member of any church; I am not a member of any religious organization; but my hand shall wither and my lips shall be sealed in eternal silence before I will ever give my official approval to any act that will stamp out the religion of Jesus Christ and establish paganism in its stead. I hope that we can meet every question that comes before us and decide whether it is right or wrong. If it is right, then let us approve it.

"I hope that I may be given the humble privilege of being classed as one of the followers of the religion proclaimed by Abou Ben Adhem. Old Ben Adhem was awakened in the night by an angel. The angel was writing in the book. Ben Adhem asked what he was doing and the angel said: 'I am writing the names of those who love the Lord.' Ben Adhem asked: 'Is my name written there?' and the angel said: 'No.' Then Ben Adhem said: 'I pray thee, then, write me as one that loves his fellow men.' The angel wrote and vanished, and the next night Ben Adhem was awakened again from his slumber. The same angel appeared, and he bore a scroll, upon which was written in letters of flaming fire the names of those who loved the Lord, and, behold, Ben Adhem's name led all the rest."

I submit that it discloses an ineradicable and ingrained simplicity of mind to tell the Senate the story of Abou Ben Adhem and apply it to one's self. But it does reveal a lack of self-consciousness and a clear self-knowledge.

Norris has had a career that has become conventional in his part of the United States. He was born on a farm in Sandusky County, Ohio, in 1861, and spent all of his early life on the farm where he was born. He learned what real, honest, grubbing work was at an age when more carefully nurtured children are being taught to cut out paper flowers and truncated cones in the kindergartens. His father died when he was a small child, his only brother was killed in the Civil War, and his mother was left in straitened circumstances. Young Norris "worked out" among the neighboring farmers by the day and month during the summer, and attended district school during the winter. He acquired enough education to become a school-teacher, and moved West. He lived in several of the Far Western and Northwestern States, and taught school in abandoned barns and chicken-houses and other queer shacks that he had to fit up with his own hands.

By what wizardry of finance this young itinerant school-teacher saved enough money to come back to Ohio and pay his way through Baldwin University at Berea, Ohio, and the Northern Indiana Normal School at Valparaiso, Indiana, even he cannot now explain. But he did, and later studied law while teaching, and was admitted to the bar in 1883. Two years later he went to Nebraska and settled at McCook.

Law and politics are virtually identical pursuits among small-town lawyers who want to "get on" in the world. Norris quickly became prosecuting attorney at McCook. He held the place three terms, and then in 1895 and again in 1899 was elected a district judge. He was on the bench, and it was as Judge Norris that he was elected to Congress in 1903. He sat in the House over nine years until 1913, when he was translated to the Senate, where he will probably remain as long as he likes. He attained a country-wide celebrity in 1910 when, on a Saturday afternoon in March as the climax of the "insurgent" movement in Congress, he caused the rules of the House to be changed in an important and essential particular; diverted from the office of the Speaker a great share of its power, and shook and humbled and defeated Mr. Cannon after a series of dramatic and exciting scenes such as are witnessed in Congress once in a generation. He never sought publicity or notoriety or claimed "leadership" because of that achievement. When he had done what he set out to do, he relapsed into the ranks. But since that day he has had to be reckoned with. He became notable, not because he was different, but because there were so many like him for whom he was articulate.

In his manner, in his processes of mind, and in his mode of living he is as simple, as plain, as direct, and as unassuming as when he was teaching the three R's in Idaho. He knows more, of course, than he did then. His mind is more mature and has broadened. His convictions, however, for the main part, are based on what he has personally known and seen and not on deductions from wide reading. He is not afraid to think and do for himself, because he has never known anything else.

Norris derives his mental sustenance and stimulation from a process analogous to cracking hickory nuts with his teeth and picking out the "goodies"

with a hairpin. He gets at the meat of a thing slowly
and by a laborious process; but he gets it, and it's all
his; he earns it. No personal animus or self-interest
has been disclosed in anything that he has said or done
in his public life at Washington. Whether right or
wrong, to all appearances he is disinterested and striv-
ing for what he conceives to be the general welfare.

Norris could not be called, as the phrase runs, "a
natural-born leader." He has never pretended to be
one; that is not his strength or the measure of his
value. He does not contend for personal preferment.
He is always a part of the irresistible mass that shows
the immovable bodies how to take a joke.

He usually does what he sets out to do and makes a
clean job of it. As they say out in Red Willow County:
"George makes good on his proposition." He is a
reassuring figure in public life in these troublous days.
He is also a darn good fellow, and I like him, and now
that you have been introduced, I hope you will like
him, too.

WASHINGTON'S HARDEST JOB

To Mr. George B. Christian, Jr., who has come out of Marion with Mr. Harding to be Secretary to the President, I can give one bit of reassurance. There is one thing he can be sure of ; he will never be bored. Something or other will happen to him every day. When he has served a term at the White House and goes out to other employment. no matter what he has to do, it will seem easy to him.

Being a President's interpreter and steersman is the most difficult and trying job in the Government service at Washington. To men who make successes of it, the subsequent rewards are great and satisfying, and even some of the failures seem to do fairly well by themselves when they resign to accept more congenial employment.

The Secretary to the President is not a private secretary, but a public secretary. His obligations to Mr. Harding's callers and correspondents are just as valid as his obligations to Mr. Harding. He must serve two masters and please both of them at peril of his head. When he is working at the job he is as busy as a Swiss bell-ringer. He must know everybody and everything. He must be able to appraise the actors on the Washington stage not only at their true value, but at their own estimate of their value. He must know what is going

GEORGE B. CHRISTIAN, JR., SECRETARY TO THE PRESIDENT

on in legislation, politics, and society, and of all the thousands who come to the White House on one mission or another he must unerringly separate the sheep from the goats. He must work all day every day and keep his temper and his health. He must always remember that when he does anything praiseworthy, the credit must go to the President and the Administration. Whenever the President makes a mistake or commits an indiscretion, the perfect secretary must offer himself as the sacrifice.

That is all Mr. Christian has to do, and for it a grateful Government allows him $7500 a year and the use of two motor cars. Also he is invited out to lunch and to dinner more than is good for him; but that can't be helped and is a part of the job.

Mr. Christian has come to the job at a time when it sadly needs to be restored to its old dimensions and authority. Mr. Wilson altered during his tenure of the White House many Washington values that had come to be accepted as permanent. He pared down the stature of many public and official figures. No figure or personality of consequence in the Washington scheme of things as it existed prior to Mr. Wilson's arrival has been so obliterated, blurred in outline, reduced in value, and decreased in functioning capacity as that of Secretary to the President. No picture in the Washington gallery offered less resistance to the effacing sponge than did Mr. Tumulty. He and the President between them made the secretaryship conform to the geometrical definition of a point : occupying a position in space but without dimensions.

We here at Washington are watching with friendly eyes to see if Mr. Christian can rehabilitate his job and restore it to its old splendor in the local scheme of things. He has yet to prove his quality. We only know of him yet what he has told us : that he is forty-eight years old — eight years younger than the President; that he was "engaged in the limestone industry in Marion County" until 1915, when he became private secretary to Senator Harding, and was then translated with his old-time friend, neighbor, and employer to the White House. That is the foundation on which he must build.

He is a gravely pleasant young man, of an even temper, apparently not easily flustered or put out or excited ; in many respects a fairly good second carbon copy of his chief. He cannot bluff his way through. He, like the President, will soon come to be known for what he is. His value, his fiber, his quality are being searchingly appraised. His relations with his chief cannot be hidden. If the President trusts him, relies upon him, gives him responsibilities, or is guided by him in any degree, a good many people soon come to know it.

If Mr. Christian ever comes to my house in the evening to smoke a pipe, I'd like to tell him about some of the figures who have gone before him and with whom I have had traffic and dealings. George B. Cortelyou was the best one I ever knew.

I would tell Mr. Christian first how we all felt when President Wilson fell ill in the autumn of 1920 and all the news from his bedside, which had become the seat of government, had to be screened through Mr. Tumulty. The importance of the office of Secretary to the President was thrown into high relief. It is a matter of public concern who fills the job.

Since Mr. Wilson was unable to transact public business in his office, it followed that his only channel of news of what was going on in the world that affected his duties and responsibilities as President was through his secretary. It is equally true that the only source of news Congress, the executive officials of the Government, and the public had of Mr. Wilson's condition, his decisions, his desires, and his attitude of mind on the several immediate, pressing public problems that came to a head was through Mr. Tumulty.

When Mr. Wilson collapsed on his return to Washington after his breakdown on his Western trip, the whole world was concerned and alarmed. The President had in his hands the strings of control of events in the making that affected the destinies and literally the lives of millions of people at home and abroad. It was not curiosity about an eminent figure, but sheer, vital, absorbing self-interest that made a startled and apprehensive world turn to the White House for exact, truthful, trustworthy news of the patient, what ailed him, how sick he really was, and whether he would get well again.

There were officials of the Government at Washington, the Vice-President, the members of the Cabinet, who would have been charged with new and complex and difficult duties in the event of Mr. Wilson's incapacity, and who were not told in the beginning anything beyond the bulletins given out for publication in the newspapers. And these bulletins were written in such language as to give rise to the gravest forebodings. Their tone and their phraseology were such as are always reserved to give warning that hope has been given up.

A clumsy, forbidding mystery was made out of the President's illness, in which sinister rumors bred like maggots. There was lacking an articulate voice at the White House, a spokesman with enough vision and understanding to perceive his obligations, not only to the President, but to the whole people, and to tell the whole truth simply and sincerely in a way that would command respect and instant acceptance. There should be no more question about the authenticity, validity, and scrupulous accuracy of a "White House statement" than there is about a Supreme Court decision.

But Mr. Tumulty was not wholly to blame. He had been cast for a rôle he was not qualified to play. I think a summary of the Washington verdict on the relations between Mr. Wilson and Mr. Tumulty would have been, "The President is fond of Joe." But that Mr. Tumulty was ever a counselor, or even a trusted confidant, there is nothing to show. The relation between the two men had become fixed at Trenton, before Mr. Wilson came to Washington, and neither was prepared to make the change when it became necessary greatly to enlarge and radically increase the power and discretion enjoyed by the Secretary.

Mr. Taft had not been in the White House more than two years before he had taken on his third Secretary. He finally found the man he needed in Charles D. Hilles. It was a happy day for Mr. Taft when Mr. Hilles came to the Executive offices for he needed a Secretary of capacity as badly as any of our Presidents have ever needed one.

A Secretary is largely measured by his tact and skill and intuition in letting in to the President only those persons whose affairs justify invasion of the Executive's time. Men have sought an appointment with the President to ask if he would allow them to test a toy motor-boat in the basin of the fountain at the rear of the White House.

One fine spring morning two Congressmen asked one of Mr. Taft's earlier secretaries for an appointment to present a delegation to the President. The request was granted. On the day appointed, the two Congressmen appeared with more than two thousand men and women. They simply overran the White House offices and grounds. Mr. Taft, with great good-nature, shook hands with about five hundred before giving up the job. His whole schedule of appointments for the day was hopelessly disarranged. A great many other persons suffered inconveniences. The two Congressmen could not be made to see that they had imposed upon the President or upon those others who had engagements with Mr. Taft. A competent and wary Secretary would have found out the size of the delegation and all about it before making the appointment.

The job of Secretary to the President has been made, and should be, as important as that of a Cabinet officer. A present-day Secretary should be more than a mere sublimated stenographer. The office has no statutory definition. One Secretary may be a good stenographer, another a politician, another a social leader, another a nonentity, another a chump. All these different varieties have flourished their brief day in Washington. The office has greatly and visibly increased in power, prestige, and importance as new burdens have been thrown upon the President and as the conception of the powers of the office of the President itself has been enlarged.

There have been twenty-eight different Presidents of the United States, and all of them had one or more private secretaries, but the list of men to whom the office has proved a "stepping-stone" to further honors and an enlarged sphere of life is a short one. John Hay, John G. Nicolay, Horace Porter, Daniel Lamont, George Bruce Cortelyou, William Loeb, Jr., and Charles D. Hilles are names that stand out from the list of those who have held the office. The others fell back into oblivion, or never emerged from it, even while they were in the White House, and their subsequent activities and exploits are unrecorded.

The enlarged dimensions of the office of Secretary to the President were marked out by Daniel Lamont when he came to Washington in the first Cleveland administration as Secretary to the President. He had been Governor Cleveland's Secretary at Albany. In Mr. Cleveland's second administration Mr. Lamont was Secretary of War. During his tenure of office as Secretary to the President, Mr. Lamont to some extent made it an added Cabinet position. His personal influence with Mr. Cleveland was on a par with that of any of the seven counselors provided by law.

After Lamont comes Cortelyou, who was confidential stenographer to Grover Cleveland, Secretary to McKinley and to Roosevelt, Chairman of the Republican National Committee, Postmaster-General, Secretary of Commerce and Labor, and Secretary of the Treasury in the Roosevelt Cabinet. Mr. Cortelyou was very nearly the ideal Secretary to the President. He had political sagacity and experience. He knew public men, he was a competent executive, and could dispose of an enormous amount of routine business without hitch or flurry. He had an intimate and detailed knowledge of the processes of government, was careful and cautious to a degree, had a manner that inspired confidence, and was always the master of himself and of circumstances. There were never "unfortunate slips" when Mr. Cortelyou was in the White House Executive offices. Everything ran as smoothly as an eight-day clock.

When Cortelyou was Secretary, every premeditated Presidential utterance was viséed and verified in advance of its publication. Every affirmation of fact was authenticated. If McKinley said in a speech that the world's stock of gold on such and such a date was such an amount, the assertion was sent to the Treasury Department for verification. Every quotation he used was looked up. Every assertion of historical fact was run down carefully. Cortelyou even ventured to rewrite and ameliorate the tone of some of the Presidential letters. This was necessary more often with Roosevelt than with McKinley.

Loeb, who succeeded Cortelyou when that efficient private secretary went into the Cabinet, left a mixed impression in Washington. While he was Secretary to Roosevelt, the newspapers continually blossomed with the headlines "Loeb Takes the Blame." It would have been the same had an archangel held the post. No man had a more faithful and devoted servant, or a more loyal and untiring assistant than Roosevelt had in Loeb. Though Loeb customarily figured in the newspapers as a sacrificial goat, he was a competent man in the post and did not allow the dimensions of the office to shrink during his incumbency. He had many and curious adventures.

Presidents from Washington to McKinley had private secretaries. When John Addison Porter came to Washington in 1897 to serve William McKinley in that capacity, he assumed the title of Secretary to the President. The next year Congress dropped the old title and appropriated money to pay the salary of a Secretary to the President.

The line of Presidential Secretaries begins with Tobias Lear and Lawrence Lewis, who served under Washington. In the beginning and even down to Garfield's time, our Presidents seem to have had a fondness for bestowing the secretaryship upon young kinsmen. Lawrence Lewis was Washington's "sister Betty's son." The letter is preserved in which the young man accepted the post:

FAUQUIER CO.
July 24, 1797

MY DEAR SIR:

I return you my sincere thanks for the kind invitation I received when last at Mount Vernon to make it my home, and that whilst there my services would be acceptable. This invitation was the more pleasing to me from a desire from being serviceable to you, and from a hope in fulfilling those duties assigned me I should derive some improvement by them.

Untutored in almost every branch of business, I can only promise a ready and willing obedience to any instruction or command you may please to give. I should have been with you ere this, but for the unavoidable detention of my servant's running away, and that at a time when I was nearly ready for my departure. I have been ever since in pursuit of him without success. The uncertainty of getting a servant or my runaway will probably detain me until 25th of August, but not a moment longer than is unavoidable.

With sincere regard for my Aunt, and family

I remain, your affectionate Nephew

LAWRENCE LEWIS

GEN. GEORGE WASHINGTON

Of Tobias Lear, President Washington's principal private secretary, fugitive glimpses are caught in the diaries of the time. When the first Senate met at New York City it presented, in the course of its business, an address to President Washington. The entire Senate "proceeded in carriages" to President Washington's house to make the presentation. Says Maclay in his diary:

"We were received in the ante-chamber. Had some little difficulty about seats, as there were several wanting: from whence may be inferred that the President's *major domo* is not the most provident, as our numbers were well enough known. We had not been seated more than three minutes, when it was signified to us to wait on the President in his levee room. . . .

"The President took his reply out of his pocket. He had his spectacles in his jacket pocket; having his hat in his left hand and the paper in his right. He had too many objects for his hands. He shifted his hat between his forearm and the left side of his breast. But taking his spectacles from the case embarrassed him. He got rid of this small distress by laying the spectacle case on the chimney piece. Colonel Humphreys stood on his right, Mr. Lear on his left. Having adjusted the spectacles, which was not very easy, considering the engagements on his hands, he read the reply with tolerable exactness, and without much emotion."

Thus early in our national life was the fashion set of criticizing the Secretary for anything that goes wrong at the White House. He should have provided more chairs for the Senators. Here is a crisply drawn picture of President Washington's secretaries in a social aspect:

"We went to the President's to dinner. The company were: President and Mrs. Washington, Vice-President and Mrs. Adams, the Governor and his wife, Mr. Jay and wife, Mr. Langdon and wife, Mr. Dalton and a lady, perhaps his wife, and Mr. Smith, Bassett, myself, Lear and Lewis, the President's two secretaries. The President and Mrs. Washington sat opposite each other, in the middle of the table. The two secretaries, one at each end. It was a great dinner, and the best of its kind ever I was at. . . . It was the most solemn dinner ever I sat at. Not an health drank — scarce a word said, until the cloth was taken away. . . . The President kept a fork in his hand, when the cloth was taken away, I thought for the purpose of picking nuts. He eats no nuts, but played with the fork, striking on the edge of the table with it."

When Mr. Hilles became Secretary to President Taft a woman in Virginia whom he did not know wrote to him to say that she knew the President had at last found the right man because of "your prompt attention and personally written reply to my letter to you endorsing the J. V. Bickford site for the new post-office at Hampton, Virginia." This same correspondent suggested that "in order to obtain the consolation of philosophy," Mr. Hilles should read Leviticus, 16th chapter: 20th to 22d verse. He found this:

"20. And when he had made an end of reconciling the holy place and the tabernacle of the congregation, and the altar, he shall bring the live goat.

"21. And Aaron shall lay both his hands upon the head of the live goat, and confess over him all the iniquities of the children of Israel and all their transgressions in all their sins, putting them upon the head of the goat, and shall send him away by the hand of a fit man into the wilderness.

"22. And the goat shall bear upon him all their iniquities unto a land not inhabited; and he shall let go the goat in the wilderness."

As usual when an apposite quotation can be found from the Bible, there is really nothing more to say.

FROM THE HOUSE GALLERY

WE are John Hicks and wife from Hicksville. We have come to the national capital to see the sights. We came on a round-trip excursion ticket that allows us five days here when this beautiful city is all abloom and June is at its best. We must see everything that is to be seen, and that means that we must carefully parcel out our time.

We go through the State, Army, and Navy buildings, and take a ride in a sight-seeing car through the residence district. We find that we must go up in the Washington Monument, visit Mount Vernon and Arlington, see them make the money at the Bureau of Engraving and Printing, go through the Treasury vaults and be allowed to hold a package containing $3,000,000 in our own hands, and — but before we go anywhere else we must go to the Capitol. In the central rotunda we are accosted by an affable and voluble guide. He has already collected the nucleus of a following, and tells us that he is just about to start on a trip "to all points of interest about the historic building." We join him. It is only twenty-five cents, and he shows you everything. We see the statues and the big pictures on the walls, and the whispering stones, and Senator La Follette emerging hurriedly from his committee room, with a statesmanlike frown on his brow, and then we are ready to go into the gallery of the House.

It isn't a bit as you would expect it to be. We all get seats in the front row of the gallery and look down on the floor of the big chamber. It is nearly empty. A little knot of men are gathered in the center of the House, and two of them are on their feet talking at one another. Sometimes their voices rise so that we can hear what they say, but we don't understand what it means. For the most part they wrangle in tones that do not carry to us. Where is Cannon? Where is the Speaker? The guide explains that the Speaker does not preside when the House is in Committee of the Whole. We don't ask him what that means, because we don't want to show our ignorance. A little gray-headed man, with a square gray beard, and wearing gold-rimmed spectacles, is in the Speaker's chair. That is Mann of Illinois, says the guide. Who is he and what did he ever do? Why, says the guide, he is the Great Objector. And what does he object to, we ask him? Everything, says the guide.

We sit there nearly an hour trying to find out what's going on. We learn why the newspapers back home do not print a detailed and comprehensive record day by day of what is said on the floor in the debates in the two branches of Congress. Here is just exactly what happened while we sat in the gallery watching the big men of the country making the laws of the land:

The House, being in Committee of the Whole House

on the state of the Union and having under consideration the bill (H.R. 71177) making appropriations for sundry civil expenses of the Government for the fiscal year ending June 30, and for other purposes:

Mr. Blank. Mr. Chairman, I ask unanimous consent to proceed for ten minutes.

The Chairman. Is there objection?

Mr. Dash. I shall have to object to that.

Mr. Blank. I ask unanimous consent to proceed for five minutes.

Mr. Dash. I shall object.

Mr. Blank. I move to strike out the last word.

The Chairman. The gentleman has already made that motion.

Mr. Blank. Then the last two words.

Mr. Dash. I make the point of order that that is not in order.

The Chairman. The Chair sustains the point of order.

Mr. Blank. I make the point of no quorum. I propose to answer this speech, and you cannot keep me from it —

The Chairman. The gentleman is out of order.

Mr. Blank. Except by resorting to technical matters.

Mr. Doe. I suggest to the gentleman from Illinois that he wait until the gentleman from California can be present, and then we will have unanimous consent.

Mr. Blank. Oh, I could not wait.

The Chairman. This discussion is entirely out of order, and the gentleman will please be seated. The gentleman from Illinois makes a point of order of no quorum. The Chair will count. (After counting.) One hundred and forty-two gentlemen are present; a quorum. The Clerk will read.

The Clerk read as follows:

Salisbury, N.C., post-office: For site and continuation of building under present limit, $50,000.

Mr. Blank. Mr. Chairman, I move to strike out the last word. Now, in view of the fact that this speech was evidently prepared in the office of the Attorney-General, I want to read what the Attorney-General thinks about the —

Mr. Dash. Mr. Chairman, I ask that the amendment of the gentleman from Illinois may be reported.

Mr. Doe. It is too late.

Mr. Dash. The amendment has not yet been reported.

Mr. Blank. I moved to strike out the last word, and I am making the motion in the usual way.

Mr. Dash. What is the last word? I ask that for the reason that the gentleman must confine himself to the subject of his amendment.

Mr. Blank. I move to strike out the word "dollars."

Mr. Dash. We cannot proceed in any other way.

The Chairman. The gentleman from Illinois offers an amendment, which the Clerk will report.

The Clerk read as follows:

Page 9, line 11, strike out the word "dollars."

Mr. Blank. And upon a motion like that to strike

out the word "dollars" it is perfectly proper to discuss the Attorney-General of the United States. I want to show what he thinks about himself. I read now from the first column on page 7561 of to-day's *Record*, referring to my criticisms of him:

And what seems strange to me is that when at last we have a strong, able, vigorous, and thoroughly in earnest Attorney-General —

Mr. Dash. I make the point of order that the gentleman is not addressing himself to the amendment. I want to say to the gentleman that it is the desire of all Members of this House to conclude the reading of this bill, and it will be concluded inside of an hour ; and if he will wait until we conclude the reading of the bill, I will have no objection to his having ten or fifteen minutes in which to address the committee.

Mr. Blank. But if the gentleman does not have objection, somebody else will.

Mr. Dash. The gentleman is a Member of the House, and he ought not to try, in violation of the rules, to delay the further consideration of this bill.

Mr. Blank. But this speech comes into the *Record* in violation of the rules.

Mr. Doe. Mr. Chairman, I ask unanimous consent that, after the consideration of the bill shall have been completed in the Committee of the Whole, the gentleman from Illinois (Mr. Blank) may have ten minutes.

Mr. Dash. I will not object to that.

Mr. Roe. I object.

Mr. Blank. I insist on my right to the floor now.

The Chairman. The gentleman from Minnesota makes the point of order that the gentleman from Illinois is not speaking in order to the amendment. The Chair will remind the gentleman from Illinois that general debate has been concluded upon this bill and that the universal rule in consideration of the bill by paragraphs is that the debate must be confined to the bill. The Chair hopes the gentleman will confine himself to the bill and that the gentleman will proceed in order.

Mr. Blank. I have much respect for the presiding officer and for his knowledge of the rules, yet I must call his attention to the fact that while the rule may be as the Chair states — and I do not promise to question that matter, because my colleague from Illinois, the chairman at the present time, knows much more about the rules than I do — but the Chair will agree with me that upon a motion to strike out the last word it is the invariable custom of the House to permit members to discuss matters that do not pertain to that paragraph.

The Chairman. The Chair is under the impression that the gentleman from Illinois is in error in thinking that. Undoubtedly upon a motion to strike out the last word it is in order to discuss the merits of a paragraph.

Mr. Blank. Then I move to strike out the paragraph.

The Chairman. Undoubtedly on the motion to strike out the last word of a paragraph it is in order to discuss the merits of the paragraph, but it is not in order in the committee, on the reading of an appropriation bill, general debate having been concluded, to discuss extraneous matters not relating to the subject under consideration at the time.

Mr. Blank. I hope the gentleman from Minnesota will not object to my speaking for ten minutes. The House will have sufficient time —

Mr. Dash. I will say to the gentleman from Illinois I will not object to his proceeding for ten minutes if that will be the end of it.

Mr. Blank. That will be the end for to-day.

Mr. Dash. I have no objection.

The Chairman. The gentleman from Illinois asks unanimous consent to speak for ten minutes to discuss the subject he has under consideration. Is there objection?

Mr. Doe. I object. I know that the Representative —

The Chairman. The gentleman will be in order; he has objected.

Mr. Blank. Then, Mr. Chairman, I ask unanimous consent at the conclusion of the reading of the bill for ten minutes.

The Chairman. The gentleman from Illinois asks unamimous consent that at the conclusion of the reading of the bill he may have ten minutes —

Mr. Doe. I object, until the gentleman from California is present —

The Chairman. The gentleman from Tennessee will suspend —

Mr. Blank. The gentleman from California is never here; he is always away making political speeches for his party.

The Chairman. The gentleman from Illinois asks unanimous consent upon the conclusion of the reading of the bill that he may have permission to address the House for ten minutes.

Mr. Doe. Mr. Chairman, I object.

Mr. Blank. I hope the gentleman will get in at the conclusion of the reading of the bill, because I shall ask for permission again.

The Chairman. Without objection, the amendment is withdrawn, and the Clerk will read.

The Clerk read as follows:

San Angelo, Texas, post-office and court-house: For site and continuation of building under present limit, $25,000.

Mr. Blank. Mr. Chairman, I move to strike out the last word. The gentleman from California is here. Now I ask for permission to proceed for ten minutes.

The Chairman. The gentleman from Illinois asks unanimous consent that he may proceed for ten minutes.

Mr. Dash. I will ask the gentleman from Illinois if he will not qualify his request and make it at the conclusion of the reading of the bill, which will be very soon now.

Mr. Blank. I should prefer to go ahead now.

Mr. Dash. I will say to the gentleman, of course it would be manifestly unfair for him to proceed for ten minutes and then deny the gentleman from California the same right, which would make twenty minutes, if made prior to the conclusion of the consideration of this bill; but if the gentleman from Illinois will renew his request of a moment ago that he may have ten minutes at the conclusion of the bill, I am satisfied there will be no objection.

Mr. Blank. I will make the request for fifteen minutes.

The Chairman. The gentleman from Illinois asks unanimous consent that at the conclusion of the reading of the bill he may proceed to address the committee for fifteen minutes. Is there objection?

Mr. Doe. Mr. Chairman, I ask also that the Representative from California be allowed fifteen minutes.

The Chairman. In that connection the gentleman from Tennessee asks that the request be modified so that the gentleman from Illinois may have fifteen minutes, and the gentleman from California fifteen. Is there objection? (After a pause.) The Chair hears none and it is so ordered.

All of this time, and the space occupied in reporting what was said, represents the efforts made by a Democratic member of the House to attack the Attorney-General. The newspapers that reported the incident at all dismissed it in a few lines. I have quoted it *in extenso* here to show how a large part of the time of the House is occupied.

One of the reasons why such a generally false impression of Congress is diffused throughout the country is the practice of the newspapers of printing only the interesting things that happen on the floor of the two chambers. When there is a good debate over some subject on which interest runs high, or when there are exciting clashes between the Democrats and the Republicans, columns of newspaper space are devoted to an account of what takes place. When the public outside of Washington reads of the House of Representatives it is always in connection with some scene or debate that is dramatic or important or picturesque and interesting. Therefore, when the average reader of newspapers comes to Washington on a visit and sits for an hour in the gallery and hears some such interchange as has been printed above, he goes away puzzled and confused.

When the guide said it was time to be going, if we wanted to climb to the dome or go in and see the Supreme Court for a little while, we told him we didn't think much of what we had seen and heard, but he told us it was not always like that. Sometimes, he said, all of the members were in their places on the floor, and there was plenty of excitement and high debate. We told him we wished that we might have seen something like that going on. The guide pointed across to the press gallery above the Speaker's chair. "There is just one sure way of knowing when something interesting is about to happen in the House," he said. "When you see the correspondents begin to come out of their own room back of their gallery and fill up their seats, then you may be sure that something is about to happen on the floor, and when you see them get up and leave the gallery, no matter how noisy it may seem on the floor, you may be sure that nothing else is going to happen for a while at any rate."

We looked across to the press gallery, but there was only one young fellow in it, and he seemed to be drawing pictures on a piece of yellow paper. When he got up, yawned openly at the House of Representatives, and disappeared through a swinging door, we went away too.

REMARKABLE MR. ADEE

WHEN the Mukden viceroy went to the station to meet Prince Tsaichen, on his way home to Peking from the coronation of King George at London, the Prince sobbed and wept because (1) England only gave him thirty-sixth place at the coronation, immediately before the "lost state" of Egypt; (2) at the King's banquet, and again at the Foreign Office banquet, he was invited without his staff, though the envoys of Japan, Europe, and America brought their suites. Moreover, the language used toward him was cold; and when he was decorated he alone (and not his suite) received an order. This, he complained, contrasted very unfavorably with that received at King Edward's coronation; and even with that (less courteous) at King Edward's funeral. Consequently he kept his blinds down all the way in the Russian train, and would not see any one. He blamed the London Minister, Liu Yuh-Lin, for not having made it clear that he was an Imperial Prince.

This never would have happened had Prince Tsaichen been visiting us. There is a reason; his name is Adee.

If you were living at Washington and held an official position of sufficient rank and importance, it might easily happen that you would be called upon to entertain at dinner some evening an ambassador, a Korean prince, a pretender to the throne of Portugal, an associate justice of the Supreme Court and a senator from Oklahoma who were not on speaking terms, an exiled Shah of Persia, the Secretary of the Chamber of Commerce of Peoria, the Assistant Fish Commissioner, a retired admiral of the Navy, and the president-general of the Daughters of the American Revolution. Assuming that they were all sticklers (and this is a safe assumption) for precedence, how to seat them would be a problem, unless you knew and were in the good graces of one certain man.

His name is Adee.

Assume that you have been elected President of the United States. One of your duties would be to write letters of congratulation to, say, the Duke of Saxe-Coburg on the birth of a son, or you might have to condone with the Duchess of Schleswig-Holstein on the death of her great-uncle, the Archduke of Something Else, or with the Emperor of Abyssinia on the sudden demise of his favorite wife. These are not little notes that may be "dashed off." There are certain fixed gradations of grief or happiness to be felt by rulers and potentates that have been carefully formulated through years of international correspondence. The President of the United States is much more grieved when the King of England loses a cousin than he is when the Crown Prince of Siam loses a son.

There is only one person among us who knows precisely how much sorrier the President is. His name is Adee.

Alvey Augustus Adee, Second Assistant Secretary of State, is a unique figure at Washington. He is the complete diplomatist. He is our only permanent official. He is the man who is declared not to exist, the indispensable person. Nobody who knows the Government at Washington can imagine the State Department without Mr. Adee. He knows what Secretary John Forsyth wrote to our Minister in London in the year 1835 about the Canadian fisheries dispute. He knows what our Minister to Portugal reported to Secretary Marcy in the year 1854 about the state of that one-time monarchy. He knows the intrigues of the Court of China. He knew before the Shah of Persia knew it himself that he was to be deposed and exiled. He knows how much money the ex-Sultan of Turkey had and where he had it deposited. He could seat a dinner party in the Imperial Court at Peking without making a mistake, or lay out a bicycle tour through Germany with equal ease and precision, and his advice on either problem would be final and authoritative.

Mr. Adee has completed thirty-five years of continuous service as Assistant Secretary of State, and forty-two years of continuous service in our diplomatic service. He was born in Astoria, New York, on November 27, 1842. His first service in the diplomatic corps was as secretary of the American legation at Madrid, to which he was appointed on September 9, 1870, and, in the absence of the chargé d'affaires, assumed the duties of that office. He remained at this post until 1877, when, because of ill-health, he returned to the United States. Shortly after his return he was appointed chief of the diplomatic bureau, which place he held until July 18, 1882, when President Arthur appointed him Third Assistant Secretary of State. President Cleveland promoted Mr. Adee to Second Assistant Secretary of State on August 3, 1886. In this capacity he served under Presidents McKinley, Roosevelt, Taft, Wilson, and Harding. Mr. Adee was appointed by President McKinley as Secretary of State *ad interim* to fill a vacancy, and he served in that capacity twelve days. He was also a witness to the signing of the Treaty of Paris, between the United States and Spain, and assumed the duties of Secretary of State in one of the most critical periods of the Chinese Boxer troubles.

Many of the diplomatic notes which have established or readjusted our relations with other nations at critical periods have been written by Mr. Adee and then signed and dispatched without alteration by the Secretary of State or the President. Mr. Adee is accredited with having invented the phrase "administrative entity" in Mr. Hay's famous Chinese note. All of the chancelleries of the world have tried to fathom and interpret this phrase, but without success. It seems to mean whatever the occasion requires it shall mean. Mr. Adee was the only man who could write a dispatch which President Cleveland would sign without changing.

This indispensable diplomatist speaks and writes

fluently French, German, Italian, and Spanish, and all the rhetoricians might go to school to him in the use of the English language. As he employs it, it is either a filmy veil, an opaque cloud, or as luminous as light itself. Among Mr. Adee's minor functions was the writing of the annual Thanksgiving proclamation of the President, until the time of President Wilson, who wrote his own; and the President's addresses of welcome to foreign ambassadors and ministers when they come to the White House to present their credentials. These the President either reads or speaks from memory at the time of the presentation. During all of Mr. Adee's service as Assistant Secretary of State it is not of record that any Secretary of State, with the possible exception of Mr. Gresham, ever took any important action without having Mr. Adee prepare his case. Secretaries Hay and Root leaned upon him heavily.

Mr. Adee's knowledge of form and precedent is genuinely believed to be all-embracing and letter-perfect. He is a singularly modest man and does his honest best to hide his light. All that is known of the value of his services and his really marvelous knowledge of diplomatic affairs becomes public property through the consistent and freely expressed praises of his superiors. So far as is known, he does not even read any of the things that are printed in praise of his work. Therefore his biographers of the press always feel at liberty to praise him as openly and unstintedly as they believe he deserves.

Mr. Adee is supposed to be deaf. It seems to be a peculiar sort of deafness that enables him to hear what he cares to hear and to remain oblivious to things that annoy or bore him. One of his biographers calls attention to another infirmity which has stood him in equally good stead in his official life. That is a temper worthy of his Scottish ancestry. This writer, who knew Mr. Adee for many years, noted of this temper: when it is calm, he is urbanity exemplified; when it explodes, let those who stand nearest look out for themselves! His underlings live in awe of this sort of demonstration after having witnessed one, and it makes some of them more careful with their work; while outsiders having frequent business with the department learn to avoid irritating importunities and other breaches of courtesy.

Now and then it is the innocent, animate or inanimate, who suffer because the guilty are out of reach. Gossip used to have it that on one occasion Adee came back to his room after a very annoying interview in the Secretary's office, and began to scatter his books and papers this way and that, now slamming a bulky volume upon the floor, now sweeping a pile of unsigned letters into the waste-basket, and otherwise reducing the top of his writing-table to a plain of desolation.

Toward the close of the outburst, a messenger entered, bearing the modest luncheon Adee had ordered before going out. Its most conspicuous factor was a large piece of pie. Reaching for that as he had reached for the laws, treaties, and correspondence which he had lately sent hurtling through space, Adee flung it straight at the messenger's head. The frightened servitor dodged, and the pie shot over him, plastering itself, in all its juicy exuberance, against the portrait of a distinguished Secretary of State of a past era which hung on the wall behind. What purports to be the mark of it is still pointed out, on the sly, to visitors. There was always an apocryphal odor about this story, and I should not wish to vouch for its truth.

Secretary Hay once said: "Adee would make a good Bible. He can begin at the creation and tell me how everything was done in the past, and wind up by instructing me in my duties as head of this department. And the beauty of it is that I shan't go far astray if I follow him."

Gaillard Hunt, who served in the State Department with Mr. Adee, tells this story: Some years ago a certain under-official in the State Department went to the Secretary of State, James G. Blaine, and asked him to appoint him to a vacancy among the assistant secretaries.

"Why," said Mr. Blaine, "it would not be doing you a kindness; you would lose the place when the administration changed."

"Why so?" asked the applicant. "Look at Adee."

"Well," said Mr. Blaine, slowly, "Adee is — Adee."

Volumes could not have said more. He stands in a class by himself, without prototype or understudy, and when he shall pass off the stage a search will have to be made for some one now unknown to play his rôle. What Mr. Blaine himself thought of him was shown in a remark he once made to a visitor who happened to enter his room as Mr. Adee was leaving it. "There goes a great man," he said.

Mr. Adee is the second man of his type who has had service in the State Department at Washington. His precursor was William Hunter, of Rhode Island, who secured a clerkship in the department in 1829, was promoted to be a chief of bureau in 1833, and became chief clerk in 1852, at a time when Daniel Webster was Secretary of State. Because there were no assistant secretaries in those days, Mr. Hunter was sometimes called upon to act as head of the department. The office of Second Assistant Secretary was expressly created for him in 1866. He held it for twenty years, until his death in 1886, when Mr. Adee succeeded him. Thus it comes about that in the entire history of our government only two men have served as Second Assistant Secretary of State. It would be, perhaps, impossible to find a parallel to that afforded by these two men in any other department of the Government.

Mr. Adee is as prized and permanent a possession of the Federal Government as is the Great Seal of State which his department is charged with keeping.

MELLON: A CERTAIN RICH MAN

DANIEL WEBSTER played a sorry trick on all Secretaries of the Treasury. He had to make a speech in 1831 about Alexander Hamilton. In the accepted phrase, he spoke in part as follows:

"Hamilton smote the rock of the national resources, and abundant streams of revenue gushed forth. He touched the dead corpse of the public credit and it sprang upon its feet."

The fat was in the fire. Webster was a man of authority and the report of what he said got about. It got into McGuffey's Fifth Reader and Hill's Rhetoric and the book from which we used to take our pieces to speak on Friday afternoons. In my book it was on the page after the piece that John Spear used to speak that begins:

> By Nebo's lonely mountain,
> On this side Jordan's wave,
> In a vale in the land of Moab —

But the picture of Alexander Hamilton smiting the rock of the national resources and torrents of revenue gushing forth is one that I have carried in my mind since I was thirteen years old. It interested me. I remembered it. And I am not the only one. That is what has made all the trouble.

It seemed so easy. From that day to this there have been associations, individuals, corporations, partner-

ANDREW W. MELLON, SECRETARY OF THE TREASURY

ships, societies, clubs, what not, all animated with the
single resolve of inducing the Secretary of the Treasury
to smite the rock of the public resources while they
stood by with pails to catch the abundant streams of
revenue that gushed forth. "Look!" they have cried;
"see what Hamilton did. Why can't you be a great
secretary such as he was? Be a patriot and give the
rock a good crack for us." Some of these men are in
Congress, others are merely citizens on foot and taxpayers. They appear to have only the vaguest idea of
where the money comes from; there is plenty in the
Treasury.

At this juncture it is given to Mr. Andrew W. Mellon, of Pittsburgh, Pennsylvania, to explain to all
these persons, who have been led astray by Daniel
Webster, that he cannot get money from a rock.

Francis Hackett has a new story of two Irishmen:

"What's Michael doing now?" one Irishman asked
another at a wayside inn.

"Sure, he's gone to work for the Irish Agricultural
Organization Society."

"Go to God! What does the like of him know about
agriculture?"

"Well, he's after picking up this job with the Bee-
keepers' Association. I think that's what he called it."

"And what is he doing with them, the poor fellow?"

"Sure, he's going up and down Ireland with a
stallion bee."

Ever since he came to the Treasury Mr. Mellon has

been explaining to Congress, to the bankers, and to the public that the Government has no stallion dollar; that it doesn't breed money; that it has no way of getting money except by taking it from the earnings of those of us who have gainful occupations. Mr. Mellon may have a stallion dollar or two working for him somewhere, for he is fabulously rich. He knows about money. He respects it. He doesn't like to see it chucked about. He hadn't been in the Treasury a week before he was writing like this in a circular letter to bankers: "...the situation calls for the utmost economy. The Nation cannot afford extravagance.... The people generally must become more interested in saving the Government's money than in spending it...."

At the end of April he was writing to the Chairman of the Ways and Means Committee of the House: "The Nation cannot continue to spend at this shocking rate.... The burden is unbearable. This is no time for extravagance or for entering upon new fields of expenditure. The Nation cannot afford wasteful or reckless expenditure.... Expenditures should not even be permitted to continue at the present rate." Mr. Mellon was very much in earnest, and when he talks about money it behooves all and sundry to stop, look, and listen, for money is his specialty. He has spent his whole life in amassing and multiplying and guarding it. He is supposed to be runner-up to John D. in the Open Money-Getting Championship, but of that I

know nothing. I am asking you to consider him with
me now in his new and public aspect as Secretary of the
Treasury, and regard his fabulous wealth only as a
background.

It may very well turn out that Mr. Mellon will have
the largest opportunity and the most onerous and responsible public service of any of the men Mr. Harding
invited to Washington to share under his direction in
the conduct of national affairs. For the next half-
dozen years, and probably for a longer period, the
Government finances will need all the skill, all the
intelligence, and all the vision that can be commanded.
The Treasury, as one of the results of the Great War,
finds itself in a novel position. It has commitments
and engagements and relations at home and abroad
that it has not faced before. It is prudent and fitting
to inquire and report about Mr. Mellon. He is the
newest of newcomers in public life. What sort is he?
The data at this juncture is incomplete, but enough is
at hand to allow for a provisional estimate and impression.

At first sight he gives no slight indication of his
proved qualities. He looks like a tired double-entry
bookkeeper who is afraid of losing his job. He gives the
instant impression of being worn and tired, tired, tired.
He is slight and frail. He sits in a chair utterly re-
laxed. He wears dark, sober clothes, a black tie, his
coat always buttoned, and in these days, when even
the office boys sport silk, his socks are black, cotton

lisle, and not pulled up as sharply as they might be. I don't mean to give the impression that he isn't neat in his attire; on the contrary, he complies so closely and rigidly to the standards of a well-dressed man that it requires a distinct effort of attention and memory to remember anything about his personal appearance. Sometimes in his office he smokes small black paper cigarettes. When they go out, he relights them and smokes them right down to the end. Not an eighth of an inch is wasted. He doesn't smoke lightly, casually, unconsciously, but precisely, carefully, consciously, as a man computing interest on $87.76 for two months and eight days at 4¾ per cent per annum.

Mr. Mellon looks as if he didn't know what fun was, and I don't believe he does. Unless I am much mistaken, the job of being Secretary of the Treasury weighs on him; oppresses him. I think he takes all business seriously, as seriously as some of those men, who are as intent as trained bird dogs on their game, take golf. He is acutely conscious of all he has to do. He does not take it easily. Apparently he has handled other people's money so long that it has made him super-conscientious. Perhaps it is only natural for a man who has so much money to regard its management and control with so much gravity and concern.

I should say that Mr. Mellon was not an outgiving person. When he shakes hands he gives you only the tips of his fingers. He is so quiet, so reticent, so reserved as to give the impression of being almost inarticulate. This effect is heightened by his diffidence of manner and his hesitant manner of speech. But he can't be timid. No man can live the competitive life he has lived in Pittsburgh, and what the railroad people call the Ohio River gateways, and be timid. But he is diffident and has an odd little hesitation in his speech ; and he does love the quiet ways.

Thanks to the foresight and forethought of one of Mr. Mellon's predecessors in the Treasury, who was also a quiet man, his office has a private entrance and exit. He can come into it and leave it by a private elevator without being seen. When he goes to Cabinet meetings, he has only to come down in his own elevator to the street level and nip across the narrow roadway between the Treasury and the White House. He is not in the open a minute before he can dart in the east portico ; then he has only to follow the long passage through the east extension under the main house and through the west extension or wing, past the latticed enclosures where the White House laundry hangs, to the back porch of the executive offices. Through the open doorway, and he steps almost straight into the Cabinet room, which is hidden by a screen. In the entire journey he is only in exposed or open territory during the brief minute that he crosses the street. For the rest of it he is in his own or Administration communication trenches.

I remember his first Cabinet meeting. All the correspondents were waiting in the anterooms and passages

of the executive offices to see Mr. Harding after the
Cabinet meeting. When the meeting broke up, Mr.
Mellon came out with the others and ran into the
crowd. He plainly didn't know what to make of it.
He didn't know what it was all about. He had never
seen such a gathering outside of any directors' meeting
he had ever attended. He didn't know any of the
correspondents. None of them knew him. The other
Cabinet men were greeted and surrounded by little
knots of men. Mr. Mellon looked as if he wanted to
slip away — and he did. He isn't used to reporters
or any method or channel or form of publicity. He is
not a public man. He is as private as a toothbrush.
He is without any sort of public experience.

From what one hears, he is just as uncommunicative
in the Cabinet room as he is outside. Mr. Harding,
who is as friendly as an Elk, I suspect finds some
difficulty in establishing a close contact with his
Secretary of the Treasury. I think I am right in saying
that he had never seen Mr. Mellon until he invited
him, at Mr. Knox's suggestion, to come to Marion. I
have heard only one story about him in the Cabinet
room.

It appears that one day the Cabinet had under discussion what should be done with one of the great
war industries plants. The immediate problem was
whether twelve or fifteen millions should be spent in
putting it in condition or whether it should be abandoned and salvaged. One after another of the men

around the table gave his judgment and opinion. Mr. Mellon sat quiet. Presently the President, at the head of the table, turned toward him and said:

"But we haven't heard from the Secretary of the Treasury. What does he think about this proposal? I should like to have his views."

Mr. Mellon was hesitant. Then he spoke up in his low, quiet, dry voice. The matter was not exactly in his department; he had not given the problem any study; he was not familiar with all the conditions and the full situation; it was a question of some importance; he did not wish to be understood as giving his final opinion unless he had opportunity to go into the whole matter more fully, but he thought he could indicate possibly what his final judgment might be, if allowed to tell what he had done in a somewhat similar and personal case. He owned a war plant that stood him about fifteen or sixteen millions, and just the other day the question had come up whether to spend that much more money on it or to wipe it off. "I told 'em to scrap it," concluded Mr. Mellon.

"Well, sir," said the man who was telling the story, "the discussion in the Cabinet ended right there. The Cabinet felt that if Mr. Mellon could afford to scrap his plant the United States Government could afford to follow the same course. When the Secretary of the Treasury does participate in a discussion he usually nails it down."

Mr. Mellon will take care of our money. That is

what he has done all his life. It is a tiring job and takes
its toll of a man. You know even on the most casual
contact that he is cautious and careful and prudent
and wary beyond all words.

He gives away oodles and heaps of his own money.
His benefactions and charities run into immense sums,
but you somehow know that he never wasted a dime.
He is acquisitive. He knows how to manage, conserve,
and breed money. I suspect that most of his dollars
are stallion dollars and earn their keep. He is a de-
veloper and a builder. He has an oil business nearly as
big as the Standard's. He is possibly the chief figure in
the steel car business. He brought the aluminum industry in this country to its present pitch.

I do not choose to make the absurd statement at
this late day that he is an exceptionally able man.
That is wholly proven, though you might never suspect it at the first or even second or third meeting. If
he is anything of an economist or statesman, if he has a
wide vision, and understanding, in addition to his
capacity for acquisition, and his qualities as a finan-
cier and banker, then he too may become a great
Secretary of the Treasury like Alexander Hamilton
and cause abundant streams of revenue to gush forth.
If he does, the Republican Party will never forget him.
Streams of revenue is its whole present quest.

McCORMICK: THE YOUNG VITAMINE

IT is a great comfort to me that nobody seems to know precisely what a vitamine is. I don't know either, but I feared that somebody interested in that sort of thing might have isolated one, studied its habits, and written its life history. In such a case it would be just my luck to have a vitamine prove wholly unlike what I think it to be. Then I would be under the necessity of withdrawing it as I now apply it as a term of description to Senator Medill McCormick. And I wouldn't like to do that, because he and the vitamine seem to me playmates and the complements of one another.

The vitamine, I take it, is chiefly noted for a certain inherent lively quality. All the people I have asked about it have agreed that "it is something like electricity." It resides in yeast cakes, in beans, and other potent food stuffs. It is also something like Kipling's Fuzzy-wuzzy in that it is all hot sand and ginger when alive, and generally shamming when it's dead. It radiates pep and energy and vitality. It is a sure cure for inhibitions and inferiority complexes. It raises morale. In fine, it is just what the doctor ordered, or, as they used to say in France, the stuff to give the troops.

Now, if, in truth, this is an accurate description of vitamines, I am amply justified in applying the term to Mr. McCormick. For all of the qualities that have been ascribed to vitamines are his in ample quantity and to a major degree. He is a live spark. Mr. Dooley said that when Beveridge entered the Senate he thereby reduced the average age of that body to ninety-seven years. Mr. McCormick's entrance has increased the energy content by one hundred per cent. He goes through life with his foot always on the accelerator and can jump from three miles an hour to sixty in the length of his own shadow.

The chief interesting thing about any power plant or body of stored energy is what use will be made of it. How will it be directed ; to what end will it be applied ? Any accumulation of power is a matter of public interest if not of public concern. It is for this reason among others that I venture to bring Medill McCormick forward for consideration and examination. Now that he is a public man with what is likely to be a long political future ahead of him, it concerns us to know what he will make of himself.

Most men come to the Senate as the capstone of their political career. McCormick as a Senator is only at the threshold of his. His real service lies in front of him. His present situation is not a reward for things done, but an incentive to accomplishment. My pleasant and self-imposed task is not to submit to you a record of the past, but the beginning of a new enterprise. A race once run is history, but a race beginning is news. It is also a betting proposition. And it creates, by the same token, an atmosphere of lively expectation.

SEN   R MEDI   RMI(

Medill McCormick comes by his vitamines naturally enough by inheritance. He is Scotch-Irish to begin with, and that is a combination of bloods that is yet to be surpassed among the sons of men. In the proper admixture it gives its happy possessor tenacity and fire and vivacity, a cool daring and a quick willingness to do anything at least once. To the hardy and canny qualities of the Scotch they add the Irish gayety, and quickness of mind and imagination. When their carburetor is so adjusted as to give them the proper mixture they are good for as many miles per gallon as any make of man we have produced.

More specifically, the Illinois Senator is descended on his father's side from one of the three McCormick brothers who came to this country and eventually founded the agricultural implement business that became the basis of the International Harvester Company. His mother was a daughter of Joseph Medill, the great editor. So that on both sides he comes of men of force and action, pioneers in their fields, men of imagination and daring. He has inherited certain of their qualities, and he has only just begun in recent years to make an orderly, constructive use of them. They have brought him to the Senate at an early age (born 1877), and after the briefest of political careers. His whole experience as an active participant in politics is comprehended in the period since 1912.

He really began as a Progressive. He stood at Armageddon and after that *débâcle* came back into the

Republican ranks. He effected that transformation with an ease and celerity and a lightness of movement that was not exceeded by any and equaled by few. He demonstrated in the transaction a real political skill and facility. He did not come back to his former associates humbly and hat in hand; nor did he come back with clamor, and truculently. He proved anew that movement can be quicker than the eye. Simply one day he was a Progressive, and when he next became audible and visible he was a Republican in good and regular standing.

Many others traveled this road after the 1912 election, but for the most part their return journey was as conspicuous as that of the men who came back from Moscow with Napoleon. They acquired what may be called certain vocational stigmata and were easily identified as ex-Progressives. Bainbridge Colby is a notable case in point, because he, instead of coming back to his starting-point, branched off and became a Democrat, thereby winning his durable and lasting sobriquet as, The Loyal Chameleon. But his case was exceptional and conspicuous.

Mr. McCormick's change was effected in the Illinois legislature, in which he served successive terms, first as a Progressive and then as a Republican. He came straight on from there to Washington as a Congressman at large from his State and after a brief experience in the House was translated to the Senate.

In his present environment he has come ahead in the

Senate Republican organization. He is a member of the Foreign Relations Committee, which is counted a reward even after long service. Senator Cullom, the last Illinois Senator who sat on it, was in the chamber twelve years before the distinction came to him. Mr. McCormick's early arrival is the most conspicuous mark by which one can judge his progress in the Senate.

His present preoccupation is with foreign affairs. He has traveled widely and over a period of years that long antedated his entrance into politics. He went to Europe after the 1920 election and before the inauguration of Mr. Harding, and met and talked with the chief political and public figures in England, France, Italy, Austria, Poland, Czecho-Slovakia, and Germany. Mr. Harding summoned him to Florida to go over with him the information he had acquired. To what extent he colored or influenced the President's mind I do not pretend to know. But he had an opportunity to do both.

I cite this instance here to indicate his sense of news and news values, which so far as my knowledge runs, no other Senator has. He has an instinct for being on the spot where things are happening; the center of interest. That implies a driving force within and a quick imaginative grasp of a situation while it is forming and before it has crystallized. It indicates an eager and alert mind.

These qualities Mr. McCormick has proved. What he has yet to prove is more important to us in his capacity as a United States Senator. He must show stability, soundness of judgment, capacity for thinking a problem through, a disinterestedness in public service for the work's sake. He must base himself firmly and solidly if he is to achieve anything enduring. He is in his first term in the Senate. He has come on with a marvelous rapidity. He has speed, and a capacity for quick action, and energy. His quick rise has proved that he can make a successful appeal to voters. He has steadied and controlled and used to some purpose since 1912 his great store of energy — his vitamines, as I have chosen to call them. But not yet has he mellowed or ripened. When he does that we shall know more about him. By their fruits ye shall know them, but I take it that means fruits in their maturity.

In his present stage of development Mr. McCormick lacks suavity; he is not finally tempered or seasoned. His methods are direct and swift. He is liked or disliked with vehemence. He does not tread a cautious or politic course in his daily relationships. He does not fear to offend. He was one of the "irreconcilables" on the League of Nations. He sometimes irritates and vexes slower and more cautious minds by his flashes and his ardent, lively temperament. He is not notably reverential and respectful to his elders and equals. I have known them to resent that.

Yet unless I mistake him he is of the type that will not be denied. He is one of the new Senators who has made his name known outside of the Senate. He has given Illinois a significance and an importance in the councils of the Senate that she has not enjoyed since Senator Cullom died after long and continuous service. Continued service is one of the requisites of effectiveness in the Senate. Whether Mr. McCormick will have that is dependent upon the people of Illinois who vote. For they after all are the final judges of the qualities and capacities he discloses in their service.

I can only number myself among the detached onlookers who would like to see him given a further opportunity to develop his possibilities. The experiment to this juncture has been interesting and justified. I want to know all there is to know about vitamines.

HUGHES: A MAN OF SUBSTANCE

CHARLES EVANS HUGHES is an ill man to write about. He is as destitute of graces, of lights and shades, of frailties and foibles, of idiosyncrasies and little personal eccentricities, of the "human interest" touch, as any man in public life. It will be easy enough to write his obituary, for his career and his achievements will lend themselves to eulogy. He has a long and fine record of things done in the public interest to be recited. He has in plentiful measure the outstanding virtues of sobriety, steadfastness, trustworthiness, honesty, industry, intelligence, capacity, application, and the will to succeed. He has been as successful in private life as in politics. He has in him the qualities that make for success in whatever he undertakes — character, an educated, trained mind, shrewdness, and common sense.

But what good is all that to me? I don't want to write his epitaph, but to try to picture the man as he is in his daily walk as Secretary of State, as taxpayer, as a citizen living at 1529 Eighteenth Street N.W., subject to colds in the head, fits of temper, and other common frailties and weaknesses of mankind. It's not easy to take hold of him. He doesn't offer any inviting approach.

I had an appointment with him the other day, and when I arrived at his office he had just gone out to lunch. The Secretary was sorry, but he had been delayed in getting away for his luncheon and would I please wait until he returned.

"And how long will that be?"

"Nineteen minutes."

"Why not make it twenty and give him time to digest it?" I asked facetiously, hoping possibly to brighten momentarily the serious and precise young functionary.

"Because the Secretary takes only nineteen minutes for lunch," replied the grave-faced youth.

Now, what can you do with a man like that? I ask you.

For so substantial and unromantic a figure Mr. Hughes has been very changeable. He has had, at least, three distinct phases since he came into public view. First, as champion of the public welfare, gas and insurance investigator, Governor of New York, and Associate Justice of the Supreme Court. Second, as candidate for the presidency. And now the third and present phase as Secretary of State. While retaining the same basic substance and qualities, he had his three periods or manners: the early, the middle, and the late.

I take it from Plutarch, by way of the admirable and never sufficiently to be commended Bartlett, that Antiphanes said merrily, that in a certain city the cold was so intense that words were congealed as soon as spoken, but that after some time they thawed and became audible ; so that the words spoken in winter were articulated next summer.

There must be something in the story, for look at Mr. Hughes. Consider what he used to be and see how he has thawed, so that now he not only gives out light but warmth. I venture to exhibit him as an exception to the rule that the metaphorical leopard cannot change his figurative or rhetorical spots. It is an extraordinary case. When Mr. Hughes first emerged and became a figure of public observation and comment

> The breaking waves dashed high
> On a stern and rockbound coast.

Mr. Hughes seemed caught in the ice-cap. He was a stiff, unyielding figure, and on the rare occasions when he tried to unbend he almost audibly creaked. A frosty man, a just man, and clearly and discernibly an able man, he was called the "Charles the Baptist," or "an animated feather duster," or "a Viking in a frock coat." With it all he inspired public confidence and public trust. In those early days he was the Black Knight in brazen armor who went about slaying monsters and dragons. Except that he didn't wear brazen armor, but a long black Prince Albert coat, and trousers that were too long. (Why will they wear their trousers in folds about their ankles when they are earnest and seeking and uplifting? It connotes a state of mind and a stage of political development. It's almost a sure sign. The stronger they are on the moral issue, the longer the trousers. It is an irrelevant social and sartorial phenomenon I have observed for years, and it has rarely failed.)

And this attire is just as uncomfortable and almost as impenetrable as brass armor. In those early days Mr. Hughes wore also a great, black, spade beard parted along the 90th meridian and combed due east and due west. His hat was silk and tall and black and shiny. He didn't take it off when he addressed the populace. He had a trick of standing back flat on his heels. This made his shoes turn up at the toes so that from the ball of the foot forward the soles did not touch the ground. He made an impressive figure. In this posture and in this attire I used to see him at the up-state county fairs in New York rousing the yeomanry. He could do it, too. That was the unexpected and the surprising thing.

He was and is a powerful exhorter. He has clarity of mind and clarity and lucidity of expression. He brought a high character and a strong, cleanly working mind to bear on fundamental questions. The State politicians of that time were no match for him. They soon knew it. They guyed his whiskers and built up the legend that he lived on an ice-peak, but it got them nowhere.

Mr. Hughes made a fight for a direct primary, and got it. He urged a Public Service Commission, and one was established. He opposed a two-cent-a-mile rate on the railroads, and it was not imposed. He opposed race-track betting, and it was stopped, and 6213 sheet-writers (or thereabouts) lost their jobs that kept them out in the open air and had to go to work in the frowsty pool-rooms. The betting at the tracks was stopped, but not for long. The whole episode proved to be a striking example of how "reforms," brought about under high public feeling and under the driving force of a strong leadership, are by mutual easement and accommodation later ameliorated and modified to suit the public demand.

The situation and the procedure was this when Mr. Hughes became convinced that race-track betting was a bad thing for the citizens of New York. The betting ring was an open place openly arrived at. The bookmakers had their stands and displayed a blackboard or large chart on which the odds were posted. The bettors handed up their money and received a ticket on which was scrawled the name of the horse they backed, the odds and the amount bet. The transaction was recorded by the sheet-writer.

Mr. Hughes succeeded in stopping that. It was made illegal. In so doing the livelihood of some, and the diversion and excitement of many others, was abruptly terminated, so, after Mr. Hughes was translated from the governorship to the Supreme Bench, acute and subtle minds were brought to bear to see if something could be done about it. It all worked out in the end to the conclusion that the blight, the curse, the evil of race-track betting lay in recording the transaction. So now the whole business is carried on with a sort of nominal furtiveness. The bookmakers became "oralists." They do not openly record the wagers they make. They give the bettor no written evidence of the sum he has laid. The circumstance that it is an oral transaction seems to make all the difference.

It may be that in time the national prohibition act will work out in some such like fashion. Perhaps if we stopped calling it "hooch," and spoke consistently instead of "medicinal bitters," the opening to a way might be found.

However, that is all aside from the point. My present disposition is confined within the narrow limits of displaying a concrete example of Mr. Hughes's power of personality and his ability while governor to sway the opinions and actions of masses of people who were not concerned one way or the other until he made them concerned. That the effect was not lasting does not invalidate the performance. The same thing has happened before and since. The great achievement of Mr. Wilson's administration as Governor of New Jersey was the enactment of the Seven Sisters Bills, as they were called. In their day they were as famous as the Seven Sutherland Sisters and as well advertised. And now they are dead and nobody knows where they are buried. The wild clematis and the tangled eglantine grow over their graves. They died of neglect and malnutrition when their papa went away to Washington on other business and left them behind with strangers who did not care.

In those days of his first emergence and participation in politics Mr. Hughes made himself a national figure. His career and his performances in his first term as governor touched the imagination of the interior. The people wanted to see him and hear him. When Mr. Taft ran for President in 1908, Governor Hughes was his most effective campaign speaker. He roused more enthusiasm than the candidate himself. I traveled with both of them that year.

Mr. Hughes made a tremendous impression. He proved himself a true spell-binder. He made rear platform speeches that were models. He sized up a crowd instantly. He never failed to know whether the assemblage in train sheds, by little way stations, at junction points, in railroad yards — wherever his train stopped — were farmers, railway workers, factory hands, or just an agglomerate of citizens on foot. He knew what to say to each special audience. He lost no time getting under way. He caught and held their attention with his first sentence. Bryan could not have done it better. There is no higher standard. Mr. Hughes talked to them as a statesman, but his divination, his adaptability, his sure instinct for the right approach were those of an experienced politician.

And then, while at the very top of his stride, while he was being widely talked about as a presidential possibility, when his political career seemed assured,

Mr. Hughes accepted Mr. Taft s tender of a place on the Supreme Bench and bade farewell to politics. So bright seemed his political prospects that the step was spoken of as a retirement. I know that men interested in public affairs in New York wrote to Mr. Hughes and chided him for what they looked upon as his desertion. I think it rather irritated Mr. Hughes that his translation to the bench should have been taken as something analogous to taking the vows and becoming a cloistered monk. At any rate, there he was and apparently settled for life. It was made pretty plain that Mr. Hughes had definitely abandoned politics and would give the remainder of his working days to interpreting the law and the constitution.

Now I come to the most curious and inexplicable phase of the Hughes public career. I wish I knew more about it. Something happened to him while he was on the bench. He suffered a sea-change. If I knew what went on deep down in his mind in those days, I should feel that I had penetrated to what the biographers like to call the "real" Hughes. But I can only tell what I know. Mr. Hughes went on the Supreme Court in October, 1910. Before the national conventions of 1912 came round, the Republican Party was hopelessly split by the Progressive secession. This became a fact at Chicago in June.

A great many people turned to Mr. Hughes as a possible candidate who could harmonize and compose the party differences. He was approached in the early spring of 1912 by men who inquired whether he would be a candidate. He made it plain that he would not. He authorized Rabbi Stephen Wise and others to make it clear that under no circumstances could his name be used. It was said for him that should the convention nominate him against his will he would decline the nomination, and the convention would have its work to do all over again.

His attitude was not based on any temporary ground of expediency or the momentary exigencies of politics, or any personal feelings for Mr. Taft who had appointed him to the bench. It was based on fundamentals, the impropriety, the bad example of a Justice of the Supreme Court returning to active politics. I think every one who talked with Mr. Hughes at that time came away with the vividly impressed belief that here was a strong, sound man with matured, reasoned convictions who could not be shaken or tempted, a man who was capable of forming clear judgments and who had come to the final conclusion that a Justice of the Supreme Court could not become a candidate or accept political office; that by the mere fact of going on the bench he had given an unspoken pledge to stay there; that such was the only possible course; that it was due the great profession of the law, due the bench, due all the people who accepted the Supreme Court as final arbiter and as one national institution absolutely isolated from the passions and the taint of politics. That was the impression. Then what happened?

In 1916 Mr. Hughes was the candidate of his party for the presidency. His foot had slipped. Explain it who can. What led him to change his mind? What were his mental processes? Who tempted him and with what arguments? What reasons did he adduce to himself? Why did he do it? I don't know. I wish I did. It was the oddest thing Mr. Hughes ever did. It was unlike him. It was a bad skid and I think he has paid for it.

I was not in the country during the 1916 campaign, but the general expert testimony seems to be that Mr. Hughes was not himself as a candidate. Something seemed to have happened to him. He appeared to have been suffering under a variety of inhibitions and complexes. He was far from hitting on all six in the old free way. After the election I was in several of the Western States and on the Coast. I was told everywhere: "If Mr. Hughes had not come out here, we could have carried the State for him. He would have been elected." This was particularly true in California, and I am persuaded from my own inquiries on the spot that it was a just and accurate conclusion.

And now, after the interlude since 1916 in the practice of the law, Mr. Hughes is Secretary of State, high in the confidence and the favor of Mr. Harding, sharing with Mr. Hoover the reputation of being one of the two "strong men" of the administration, and happier and sunnier and warmer and more responsive than any one has ever seen him.

It is an entirely new Hughes. The big, black, formidable spade beard is gone, and there is now a soft, white, rounded one, a mere buttonhole bouquet of a beard in place of the old impenetrable privet hedge. Gone, too, is the old long-tailed coat and the high shiny black hat. He is a great surprise to those persons who believed that he was ice-bound eight months in the year. As a matter of record Mr. Hughes is more friendly and flexible and easy in his demeanor than he has ever shown himself before.

He will tell the world that he likes his job. He fairly revels in it, and is as enthusiastic as the little boys before Christmas who believe in Santa Claus. His enthusiasm is contagious. It has affected the newspaper correspondents who regularly attend his daily "conferences," as they are called. They did a thing the other day that has never happened before in this town. The usual exchange of questions and answers having come to an end, Mr. Hughes left the room and returned to his office. Within a minute or two he came bursting back all aglow and with a paper in his hand. It was a dispatch he had found on his desk. It was news; good news, and Mr. Hughes, all bubbling, read it out loud to the assembly.

They cheered him. They actually warmly and

spontaneously applauded the performance. It was obviously so unpremeditated, so genuine, and so took them all in as interested participants, so made them a part of the enterprise, that they gave him a hand for his quick recognition of their interest and their point of view.

Whether Mr. Hughes will be a great Secretary of State I won't venture to guess. He has made a good start. He is at his ease and functioning without friction. He seems to be freed of his late inhibitions, and certainly he appears extraordinarily happy and content. It has been so long since there has been a real Secretary of State in Washington that Mr. Hughes looms up like another Pike's Peak, but it is much too early to form a judgment. About even so steadfast a man as Mr. Hughes, you never can tell. He is doing all that lies in his power to retrieve the prestige that he lost in his essay toward the presidency, and he is acquiring a great stock of public good-will. And he has got what J. Pierpont Morgan said was the best security for the loan of a million dollars — character.

LODGE: THE VERY BEST BUTTER

To be a Cabot among us is to have come over with the Conqueror. It is only fair. There is even a sort of poetic justice in it. The first of the line was John or Zuan Cabot, an Italian. He didn't have much luck. He was the first of the early tide of immigrants to reach the mainland of North America. He didn't know it. He thought it was an island, or, at any rate, the King who sent him did. He struck straight across the western ocean from Bristol with every chance in the world of landing at Boston, which would have been wonderful good fortune for everybody concerned. Instead, by a perverse fate, he touched on the coast of Labrador.

"This Venetian of ours who went in search of new islands is returned," wrote an Italian in London to his brother at home; "his name is Zuan Cabot, and they all call him the Great Admiral. Vast honor is paid him, and he dresses in silk. These English run after him like mad people." The account book of Henry VII contains the precise entry: "To hym that found the new isle 10£." Say, $35.50 at this day's rate of exchange, but, of course, as we are so often told, money went further in those days.

But interest in Cabot and his voyage soon died out.

SENATOR HENRY CABOT LODGE

It only goes to show that, even in those early, simple days, the public was fickle. It doesn't always recognize true merit, or, recognizing it for a moment, doesn't cling to it and perpetually sing its praises. And so it came about that this mainland of ours which Zuan Cabot was the first to touch was named "by an obscure German professor in a French college, after an Italian navigator in the service of the King of Portugal." Cabot's name is not connected with or given to any town, river, state, or mountain in the New World.

For us and our children there is only that perishable monument, Henry Cabot Lodge, to preserve and keep alive the name. He is the only Cabot we know. There may be others, but we plain people of the hills and valleys do not know them. Our Cabot is Henry Cabot. So far as we are concerned, he is the nationally advertised national product and all others are imitations. We ask for "the scholar in politics" and take no substitutes. The genuine cannot be mistaken. It cools the blood and is a sovereign antidote in cases of Democracy, curing even the most virulent cases of Wilsonism, in one to five days. Take a little acid for thy humor's sake.

I don't know whether or not Henry Cabot Lodge is a kinsman and descendant of Zuan Cabot. It doesn't really matter. They are spiritually akin, at any rate, have had somewhat the same experience, and Mr. Lodge has kept the Cabot name a bright beacon light in a hurried world given to forgetfulness of the brave names of old. I do not want Cabot Lodge forgotten as Zuan Cabot has been.

I wonder if by any chance Henry Adams has set down about Mr. Lodge the permanent record for posterity. There has been no man of our time more competent to appraise or more deft and adept in reducing to words the terse truth about Mr. Lodge. In his autobiography Mr. Adams has limned a little portrait of the Massachusetts Senator which, I suspect, will stand the test of many years without fading or losing its values:

"Roosevelts are born and never can be taught; but Lodge was a creature of teaching — Boston incarnate — the child of his local parentage; and while his ambition led him to be more, the intent, though virtuous, was —...restless. An excellent talker, a voracious reader, a ready wit, an accomplished orator, with a clear mind and a powerful memory, he could never feel perfectly at ease whatever leg he stood on, but shifted, sometimes with painful strain of temper, from one sensitive muscle to another, uncertain whether to pose as an uncompromising Yankee; or a pure American; or a patriot in the still purer atmosphere of Irish, Germans, or Jews; or a scholar and historian of Harvard College —...standing first on the social, then on the political foot; now worshipping, now banning; shocked by the wanton display of immorality, but practicing the license of political usage; sometimes bitter, often genial, always intelligent — Lodge has the singular merit of interesting....He betrayed the consciousness that he and his people had a past, if they dared but avow it, and might have a future, if they could but divine it."

If I had any discretion, I would close this paper right here and not attempt to enlarge upon or amplify that rich bit of spirited condensation, but there have been brave men since Agamemnon as well as before. I can, perhaps, point out some of the deft strokes of the Adams portrait and indicate and emphasize some of the larger values. For Mr. Lodge is a very special sort of person. He really is a figure apart in the Senate, and, whether the other Senators acknowledge the fact or not, they do allow him a place of his own. He is one of the personalities.

Strangers in the galleries always ask to have him pointed out. There is an atmosphere about him of tradition, of legend, myth — what you will. He retains the singular merit of interesting. But when the eager questioners in the gallery ask each in his own way upon what meat doth this our Cæsar feed, nobody seems to have a precise or definite answer. Yet Mr. Lodge always plays a conspicuous part in the Senate transactions, or in such of them as interest him. His seat is always near the top of the table. He is the nominal and titular "leader" of the Senate, yet he has no followers. He is not a natural leader, but one by virtue of his position in the Senate scheme of organization. To be quite blunt about it, he is too finicky.

I do not think that even his ardent admirers concede him a serene and lofty mind or a wide vision. Nor is he a man of quick and wide sympathies, of a big, open, generous heart. While his intelligence is everywhere conceded, other qualities and attributes are lacking that, had he possessed them, would have enabled him to become such a figure in the nation as some of his great predecessors.

It is quite true that Mr. Lodge has never made the most of himself; has never taken advantage of his abundant opportunities. He might have been a statesman of the first flight if the real right stuff had been in him, instead of a partisan, practical politician. Massachusetts is habituated to statesmen. She has produced them. She knows what they look like. She knows their habits. She is willing to allow them their freedom, their independence; not to tax them with petty, political chores; to grant them ample space and charter for disinterested, constructive public service on the highest plane they could achieve.

It is rather a pity that Mr. Lodge never made anything of, never exploited or employed, the franchise for development that his State gave him so many years ago. As Mr. Adams says, he never knew which pose to take, which foot to stand on. He has shifted from one to the other, and so it follows that he has never left the ground. He has stayed with the politicians, or, to quote again Mr. Adams's admirable and telling phrase, "shocked by the wanton display of immorality, but practicing the license of political usage." That is comprehensive enough to be an epitaph.

Mr. Lodge has been both fortunate and unfortunate in his career. Fortunate in that early in life the legend was built about him of "the scholar in politics." It was so persistently repeated that it has become a sort of trade-mark. In the beginning it was apparently a way of saying that Mr. Lodge was a superior person ; that he was unlike other politicians. And undoubtedly he was. He had great early advantages. He was born among the socially elect of his community. Even before he had a present, he had a background.

From his early youth he consorted with what the March Hare has enduringly called the very best butter. He was amply educated, not only in school and college, but by his environment and associations. His bread-and-cheese problem had been settled for him before he was born. Public life was open to him on the easiest, pleasantest terms. If he desired and had it in him to be a statesman, to make and leave his mark on the public life and public affairs of his generation, he had only to commence.

There was an immense pride in and store of good-will for him in his own State. The voters there have never checked or interrupted his career. He has been continuously in the State and National Legislature since his youth. Given the tools, he has never been denied a proper workshop for their use. And always there has been thrown about him this friendly legend of "the scholar in politics."

Only the other day I asked a man in Boston to tell me something about Mr. Lodge and his career. I sought another and more intimate viewpoint than my own. This is what he instantly told me: "Lodge's history is a part of the history of his country." There it is again, the tired editorial touch, the worn, rounded formula, the easy judgment, the ready-to-wear phrase. I suppose Mr. Lodge's history is a part of the history of his country, but so was Dr. Mary Walker's, and John L. Sullivan's, and the Dalton boys', and Mrs. Jeannette Bloomer's, and the man's that struck Billy Patterson, and heaps and heaps of others, but that sort of thing gets you nowhere.

I think we have the right to apply higher and more critical standards to Mr. Lodge. His has been no Horatio M. Alger, Jr., career. He has had no vicissitudes to encounter, no obstacles to overcome. He was launched full-panoplied on a sea of good fortune, under the happiest prophecies, and those prophecies have never been popularly revised. Indeed, by some subtle transmutation they have become popular appraisals, possibly through sheer iteration. In that Mr. Lodge has been fortunate.

But has he been really fortunate? Hasn't he had some of old Zuan Cabot's hard luck? Hasn't he, too, touched the austere coast of Labrador? Does he suspect the great fertile mainland he has so narrowly missed? Will his performance stick; will it prove a permanent, enduring thing, or will it be clouded in the obscurity of the eleventh man, the unfortunate who has played his game with some skill and distinction, but, when the final appraisal came to be made, just missed getting in the ranking ten? That is something for posterity to decide in the intervals of paying off the Liberty Bonds.

In his autobiographical sketch in the "Congressional Directory" Mr. Lodge gives his profession as that of literature. I think, too, it is his true avocation. He has an agreeable style, a well-stored mind, a distinct viewpoint. And that last, a distinct viewpoint, he has not always had in politics. He has not always known whether to cry with Miranda,

> How beautiful mankind is! O brave new World!
> That has such people in't:

or, like Emerson's "fine young Oxford gentleman," declare,

> There's nothing new and nothing true and no matter;

or, to complain with the young Hamlet:

> The time is out of joint; O! cursed spite
> That ever I was born to set it right.

Somewhere in Mr. Lodge's own writings is this sentence: "He, whose mournful incapacity for the production of new ideas has come sharply home to him, has the added pang of knowing how eagerly he thirsts for these new ideas from others and how much his ability to recognize an old idea has been developed and increased." This may or may not have a wistful auto-biographical significance. I don't pretend to know. I came across it and copied it down. It is a good sentence, at any rate.

If Mr. Lodge had devoted himself to literature with a single mind; if he had been content to be a man of letters, he would be a clearer, stronger figure against the national horizon than he is to-day. Or, if he had given to politics the disinterestedness, the sweep of interest, the broadness, the soundness of method that he brought to his literary work; if he had not "practiced the license of political usage"; if he had not thrown in his lot with the partisan, practical politicians, there would be another story to tell of him.

His political life has brought him nothing real. I take his own telling; his own record as he made it himself for the "Congressional Directory." On the side of letters and history and scholarship he sets it down that he wrote : "The Land Law of the Anglo-Saxons"; "Life and Letters of George Cabot"; "Short History of the English Colonies in America" ; "Life of Alexander Hamilton"; "Life of Daniel Webster" ; edited the works of Alexander Hamilton in nine volumes; "Studies in History" ; "Life of Washington," 2 volumes ; "History of Boston" ; "Historical and Political Essays" ; "Hero Tales from American History" ; "Certain Accepted Heroes," and other essays; "Story of the Revolution," 2 volumes ; "Story of the Spanish

War"; "A Fighting Frigate," and other essays;
"Early Memories"; "One Hundred Years of Peace";
"The Democracy of the Constitution"; in addition to
two collections of speeches and addresses.

Now, quite aside from the quality of all this writing,
the mere quantity is a solid achievement. It has been
recognized as such. He has received honorary degrees
from Williams, Yale, Harvard, Brown, Clark University, Amherst, Union, Princeton, and Dartmouth.
He belongs to learned societies that recognize scholarship, culture, and intellectual attainment : The Massachusetts Historical Society; The Virginia Historical
Society; The Royal Historical Society of London;
The American Antiquarian Society; The American
Academy of Arts and Letters; and others that I will
not take the space to recite.

Against this body of sound and solid work and these
honors in the field of literature and scholarship, what
has Mr. Lodge to set down in the way of honor and
distinction that politics has brought him? I quote the
recital he himself has made: member of the Alaska
Boundary Commission; permanent chairman of the
Republican National Convention in 1900 and 1908;
chairman of the Committee on Resolutions of the
Republican National Convention of 1904 and 1916;
temporary and permanent chairman of the Republican
National Convention of 1920 ; two terms in the Massachusetts Legislature; three terms in the House of
Representatives at Washington; and United States

Senator since 1893. Mr. Lodge sets down no record of his enduring achievements and constructive, creative work as a national legislator, and neither shall I. I would be at a loss, as presumably he was.

Now it seems to me that this dual record of literature and politics convicts Mr. Lodge of not having made the most of his great opportunities. The amplitude of the provision that was made in youth for him to become a statesman, the freedom from material cares and burdens, the extraordinary and wholehearted and continuous support given him by his State, the happy fortune of an intelligent and appreciative constituency that preferred, at any rate in the Senate, statesmen to politicians — all these blessings, I venture to submit, he has not taken full advantage of.

It will not be denied that he is a convinced and narrow partisan, that he has consistently "practiced the license of political usage." His contributions to letters and to learning have been obscured by his record as a politician. That is for him a misfortune. He has not played his hand well ; as it might have been played by a man of larger stature, of larger vision. He should have led out his trumps.

WHY NOT KNOX?

ACUTELY aware as I am of the irrelevance of the discovery, I will no longer refrain from communicating and making public record of the fact that one pair of Mr. Taft's trousers would make two suits and a short spring overcoat for Mr. Philander Chase Knox. Mr. Taft is a large package. Mr. Knox is a small package. Yet they have one thing in common. Each of them has been offered a seat on the Supreme Bench three times. Such a thing never happened to any other man in our history. It is a record.

Mr. Taft accepted the third proffer. Mr. Knox declined every time. He had an idea at one time that some day his mail would be addressed to the White House, and it was not then the practice of the Republican Party to select its presidential candidate from the Justices of the Supreme Court. Later the experiment was made, but it hardly will be repeated.

Of the three offers of a place on the highest court that came to Mr. Knox, two were made by President Roosevelt and the third by President Taft. Here are the letters, never before published, I believe, in which the honor was tendered Mr. Knox by Mr. Taft, and Mr. Knox's reply:

THE WHITE HOUSE
WASHINGTON
November 29th, 1911

DEAR MR. SECRETARY:

I have been talking over with Senator Oliver the regret I had that Pennsylvania did not offer a lawyer for the vacancy on the Supreme Bench. He said, Why not Knox? To which I replied that I supposed you would not accept the position. I don't know what I could do to fill your present place if you would accept, but my interest in the Court would lead me to put aside all other considerations to secure your service on that great tribunal.

I write to offer the place to you formally because, if you do not accept now, as you did not when President Roosevelt offered it, you may have in writing evidence of what two Presidents have thought of your ability to fill the highest place that lawyers can aspire to. Don't think for an instant that I could fill your present place. I don't know how I could fill it. In every way your service has been most gratifying and comforting. Without you at the head of the family, the circle would be desolate ; but for the reasons stated above, I wish to offer the Supreme Bench to you again.

(Signed)   WM. H. TAFT

November 29th, 1911
DEPARTMENT OF STATE
WASHINGTON, D.C.

DEAR MR. PRESIDENT:

I am deeply grateful to you for the offer to nominate

SENATOR P. C. KNOX

me for the place upon the Supreme Court made vacant by the death of Mr. Justice Harlan.

To be thought worthy to fill so eminent a place by one so conspicuously fitted to make discriminating choice is in itself an honor rare and distinct.

I shall omit reference to the reasons which have influenced me in the past in determining that such abilities as I may possess for the public service do not suggest a judicial career, beyond saying that my exalted conception of the judicial function is not satisfied by any contemplation of my own aptitudes.

Therefore, with the sincerest thanks for your expressions of confidence and over-generous appraisement of my present service, I will ask you, dear Mr. President, to accept this as an evidence of my unwillingness to sever our present most agreeable official relations.

Faithfully yours
(Signed)   PHILANDER C. KNOX

While Mr. Knox must share with Mr. Taft the distinction of being one of the two men three times offered an associate justiceship on the Supreme Bench, he is the only person in the history of the United States who has ever been called away from a performance of a musical comedy at a theater to have such an honor thrust upon him. On a sunshiny November afternoon, in 1907, Mr. Knox resolved to do a thing he had not done in many years; to go to a matinée at a local playhouse of Washington. In the middle of the second act, an usher came tiptoeing down the aisle with a whispered message that Mr. Knox was wanted at the White House at once. There was nothing to do but obey the summons.

Outside the theater Mr. Knox learned that President Roosevelt had been trying to find him at the Capitol and at his residence, and that the messages from the White House were urgent. The Senator hastened across Lafayette Square and into the President's office. There Mr. Roosevelt told him that he wanted him to accept the vacancy caused by Justice Brown's retirement. Mr. Knox declined, leaving the way open for Attorney-General Moody to scale the dizzy height. When Justice Shiras retired, the tender of his seat in the Supreme Court was made to Mr. Knox by President Roosevelt. Mr. Taft had previously declined both of these seats before they were offered to Mr. Knox.

At mean low water the crown of Mr. Knox's head rises not more than five feet six inches above sea level. He is a small receptacle, but tightly packed, sharing with Mr. Elihu Root the distinction of being one of our most highly finished domestic products. Because he is so highly finished, Mr. Knox is a difficult man to describe. He offers no point of attack. This does not mean that he presents a forbidding front. His personality is not known to any large number of public men in Washington.

Mr. Knox chooses his friends with the careful discrimination of a collector. In his hours of ease he is a teller of good stories, and a most companionable man. In his daily walk he is not austere, but no one ever saw anybody — even a Senator — clap him jovially on the back and call him "Phil." Mr. Knox looks more like a French or Italian churchman, whose avocation is diplomacy and statecraft, than an American politician. There is shrewdness in the distinctive droop of his keen eyes. His face is an immobile mask which effectually conceals his thought.

Every person who is born great, who achieves greatness, or who has greatness thrust upon him owes certain things to his biographers. Chiefly, he should be born of poor but honest parents, and from his infancy right through his career he should attach readable anecdotes to his name and fame. But what is one to do if one's hero is Philander Chase Knox? Mr. Knox has never conformed to any of the established rules laid down by the Biographers' Union. He began wrong.

As perplexing as anything else in Mr. Knox's rise in the world is the discovery that he has not adhered to the conventional maxims and precepts for attaining success. He did not have the inestimable advantage of being born of poor but honest parents. He has overcome this disadvantage of his early youth. But he has been no more successful than the average safety-deposit vault in attaching anecdotes to his career and public service.

In despair one compares him with a Yale lock for inherent secretiveness and ability to withstand assault from those who would pluck out the heart of his mystery. The real Knox, the inner Knox, is as difficult of access and as hard to describe as the mechanism of a hunting-case Swiss watch locked up in a burglar-proof safe.

Once upon a time a writing man came over to Washington and spent a day in the White House with Mr. Roosevelt. Then he went away and wrote a whole book about the President based on that day's observations. Men have known Mr. Knox for years and years, and could not if their lives depended upon it write of him one thousand words of intimate characterization. Once, long ago, somebody seeking his anecdotal "side" wrote that he was a confirmed and brilliant devotee of the game of billiards. As a matter of fact, he has never played the game. It is a problem with him to-day whether he shall become an expert at billiards, or issue a sweeping denial of the stories that make him one.

Mr. Knox in the Senate Chamber is always a curious and interesting study. A certain fastidiousness of mind, coupled with a habit of aloofness, keeps him out of the running cross-fire of debate. A running cross-fire of debate in the Senate is usually a mild and gentle affair. It lacks the cut-and-thrust and rough-and-tumble features of a general debate in the House of Representatives. It is nearly always conducted with marked decorum and dignity, but even in these circumstances Mr. Knox seldom participates. A curious sameness marks his participation in debate. He usually rises to correct some misstatement of fact. Facts are Mr. Knox's specialty. His precise knowledge accounts for a large measure of his success.

It is not of record that Mr. Knox has ever said or done a foolish thing in his public career. He carefully counts his words for public consumption. When a man becomes accustomed to receiving large sums of money for his opinions, he becomes chary of venting them loosely. Mr. Knox is not sensational. He has never coined but one phrase, or, more precisely, given a new application to an old phrase, that has met with temporary but widespread popularity. After the Northern Securities case had been decided in favor of the Government, capital was alarmed, and the then Attorney-General promised that the Department of Justice would not "run amuck" against great corporations. The phrase was quickly caught up and had its brief day.

Mr. Knox, as Secretary of State in Mr. Taft's Cabinet, was paid a salary of $8000 a year. Each of the other members of the Cabinet was paid $12,000. Behind the discrepancy lies the only known instance on record where Mr. Knox was caught napping. One night, when it was already known far and wide that he was to head Mr. Taft's Cabinet, Mr. Knox was reading in the library of his house in Washington. A servant brought in the card of a newspaper correspondent. The visitor was at once shown in. Without preface he said :

"Senator, are you familiar with paragraph 2, section 6, article 1, of the Constitution of the United States?"

Senator Knox was accustomed to being regarded as an oracle concerning the provisions of the Constitution. He had heard himself referred to hundreds of times as "one of our greatest Constitutional authorities." Eminent lawyers had consulted him on knotty Constitutional problems, and paid him well for his opinion. Perhaps he had come to believe that the Constitution held no surprises for him. He was destined to receive one of the greatest shocks of his well-ordered life. To the correspondent's inquiry he responded:

"Why, certainly, I have read that paragraph many times, but I can't remember its provisions without looking it up."

"Will you be good enough to read it now?"

"Of course," replied Senator Knox. "I'll be glad to. What do you want to ask me about it?" And he picked up a copy of the Constitution from his table and read:

"No Senator or Representative shall, during the time for which he was elected, be appointed to any civil office under the authority of the United States which shall have been created, or the emoluments whereof shall have been increased, during such time; and no person holding any office under the United States shall be a member of either House during his continuance in office."

"Even then the point didn't strike me," said Mr.

Knox afterwards. "I looked up at my friend waiting for him to tell me what he wanted me to elucidate for him.

"'Well,' he said, 'doesn't that prevent you from becoming Secretary of State in Mr. Taft's Cabinet?'

"Then I saw it. I was never more astonished in my life. Of course it did. As one of the Senators from Pennsylvania I had been present and had voted when the salaries of the Vice-President, the Speaker of the House of Representatives, and the secretaries of the Executive Departments were increased to $12,000 a year. I not only voted for the increase in pay, but against all the amendments that sought to overthrow the proposed increase. The increase was carried in the Legislative, Executive, and Judicial Appropriation Bill providing for the fiscal year of 1908. I'd forgotten all about it."

Other experts on the Constitution in the Senate and House sought in vain to discover some loophole or roundabout method by which Mr. Knox might legally be paid the same salary as other Cabinet members. But no way was found, and it was determined to put back the salary of the Secretary of State at the old figure, $8000 a year, from which it had been increased. Not until March 4, 1911, would Mr. Knox's term as Senator have expired ; and until then he had to content himself with a salary $4000 less per annum than his colleagues received.

Mr. Knox's ineligibility was brought to the attention of Washington by the correspondent of a Buffalo newspaper, and for many days the Capital was inclined to find a huge joke upon Elihu Root, President Taft, and Mr. Knox himself. It seemed to the layman that three such Constitutional lawyers and jurists should have been familiar enough with the Constitution to foresee the contingency before it was pointed out to them. Mr. Knox had to endure much chaffing on his lack of knowledge of the venerated instrument he has expounded so learnedly on the Senate floor.

Mr. Knox has been a Washington figure since 1901, when he left his law practice to become McKinley's Attorney-General. Apparently finding the environment congenial, he has been in the Cabinet or in the Senate ever since. After McKinley's death Roosevelt continued him as Attorney-General and Taft made him Secretary of State. Mr. Knox has either got a season ticket or knows the right people in Pennsylvania politics, for between Cabinet jobs he comes to the Senate with a sureness and ease that indicate perfection of arrangements at home.

He had his sixty-eighth birthday in May, 1921, but he apparently has taken out a writ of injunction, or what not, against the usual ravages made by the years, for he seems as fit and peppery and full of juice as ever he was. He sits up and takes his nourishment with the best of them. He still cocks up his tail feathers and can be as irascible and as assertive as he was ten and more years ago when he used to stand up to

Mr. Roosevelt. He was one of the few men (Elihu
Root was another) who "talked back" to Mr. Roose-
velt. There used to be a story current that one day
when the President asked the advice of the Attorney-
General on a problem that was then pressing, Mr.
Knox replied gravely

"I am sorry that you have asked for my opinion,
because up to the present time your proceedings have
been free from any taint of law."

That sort of thing. Mr. Roosevelt once wrote of Mr.
Knox in a private letter: "He standing for the law,
and I for rude and primitive justice."

To me there is a certain humor in the circumstance
that Mr. Knox laid the foundation of his career and
his future as an admiralty lawyer in, of all places in the
world, Pittsburgh. That inland town seems such an
odd place in which to become a rich and successful
practitioner of maritime law. But when Mr. Knox set
up his practice there the tonnage passing through the
port of Pittsburgh was greater than that of any other
American port. In the beginning his previous experience in the office of the United States District Attorney
and acquaintance among river men and shipping interests turned the admiralty business of that region in his
direction. From that it spread and grew and became
diversified and very profitable.

The impression I want to leave with you is of a
steadfast, moderate, alert-minded man, keen and
quick in his insight, thorough and deliberate in his

mental operations, and with a native gift, which has been cultivated, for the underlying philosophy of the law. He is not long-winded; he doesn't chatter. He has a capacious, acute, and subtle mind. Ever since he became a public man he has had to be reckoned with. He is an outstanding figure in the Senate to-day, and would be even a larger factor if he chose to work harder; but he doesn't. He is through with hustling and the hurly-burly. He has gone his full distance, he knows it, and so he takes it easy.

In sum: An able citizen, at ease and enjoying the fruits of his labors.

HOOVER: THE FRIEND OF ALL CHILDREN

THE truth about the sort of man Herbert Hoover is lies somewhere between what the Belgians think of him and what Senator Reed and some of his other critics say of him. He is neither a demigod nor a false alarm, but the Belgians have got a better line on him and are nearer right than his critics will publicly admit. It suits the purposes of the Missouri Senator and some others to pretend to believe that Hoover is a sort of footnote to a duke, a hybrid English product out of Ouida or The Duchess, a languid dweller in "palaces" attended by flunkeys in red plush breeches.

"And, laughing lightly, Bertie Cecil dipped his tawny mustaches in a beaker of Chambertin."

That sort of thing. There never was a more grotesque and ludicrous misconception about any man. Had you gone along Hornton Street, Kensington, in London, any time prior to 1914, and asked the policeman on the beat, or the passing postman, "Who lives in The Red House?" I'll lay the price of an inner tube against a gallon of gas that either of them would have replied, "An American gentleman, Sir. Something in the City, I think. 'E keeps himself very quiet, Sir."

That vague London phrase, "Something in the City," covered Mr. Hoover's identity like a blanket prior to the war, except among mining engineers and mining men. He was, so far as the world at large is concerned, an unknown, though rich and successful young man.

It also suits the purposes of some persons to pretend to believe that Mr. Hoover's present stature and the lengthy shadow he casts is the creation of press agents. It is sheer courtesy that prompts me to say of these that it suits their purposes to pretend to believe these things about Hoover. I will not be so ill-natured as to do them the injustice of accepting these fables as their honest beliefs. There never was an absurder libel than this one that Hoover was made by his press agents. It has been just the other way about. No press agents erected Mr. Hoover. He, on the other hand, has enlarged the professional reputation and increased the income and earning capacity of more than one press agent. He gave them something real to work on and with ; material with an appeal to public sentiment and public imagination.

Most of the talk about Hoover and his press agents and his craving for publicity is the hard-wrung and bitter cry of envy. Stated broadly, all men in public life and at the head of large public enterprises want publicity. They seek it as a great part of their reward. They are willing to pay liberally for it in cash. It is not Mr. Hoover's press agents, but the success that has attended their efforts that started the baying of the pack.

It is in order, too, to observe, as bearing on Mr.

HERBERT HOOVER

Hoover's qualities and capacity and present stature, that the enterprises in which he has been engaged, and which have brought him so much publicity, have not been furtive ones. It was essential to the feeding of Belgium and occupied France and the later relief work in Central Europe that the whole world should know the problem and how it was being solved and treated. It was absolutely essential that the whole world should take an active personal interest in it. The necessary thing was to arouse a wide interest, to inflame the imagination and enlist the good-will and active participation of the world. Otherwise Belgium would have starved as Russia has starved and as China has starved. Publicity was a tool and used as a tool. It was equally true of the Food Administration job after we got into the war. There were no laws to enforce wheatless days and meatless days and heatless days and gasless Sundays. They were enforced by an educated public sentiment created by an intelligent publicity.

Yet, oddly enough, all this flood of publicity has left Hoover's personality as unknown as it ever was. It was Hoover's public business that got the publicity. Hoover's work, Hoover's problems, Hoover's methods in solving those problems are fully known. He took a chance when he invited the world to participate and look on when he took up the Belgian business, for if that had been a fiasco he would have been one of the most spectacular failures in all history. The Hoover publicity has not disclosed and revealed the Hoover personality. People still come to Washington and ask, "What sort of fellow is this man Hoover? What is he really like when you come to know him?"

Well, to tell the truth, I don't know that I have ever come really to know him. He is one of the shyest, most sensitive, most modest, most inarticulate of men in his private relations. If it were not for his known public achievements, I do not think I should ever suspect him of great or exceptional capacities. He talks very little, and then only by fits and starts. He does not say bright, clever, or startling things. He has no gift at phrase-making or brilliant or improvised characterization. He can make himself interesting, however, when the mood takes him.

I heard him talk one night about traveling in the interior of China in the long ago before the Boxer troubles. It was as fascinating and enthralling a narrative as I ever heard. Simply told, full of light and color, keen and salient observations and savored with humor. That was a rare instance within my own experience.

Then one day a door was opened to me by a child, and it has led me to believe that children know Hoover sooner and better than grown-ups; that he reveals himself to them, and throws down all the barriers that his shyness erects against the world of adults. I am indebted to Miss Jean Kellogg, the young daughter of Vernon Kellogg, for opening the door. She told me one evening, with shining, dancing eyes and glowing cheeks, of a dam she and Mr. Hoover and Allan (Hoover's son) were building across some stream. She told me of Hoover, wading in the water "with all his clothes on" and wet and muddy to the arm-pits, as he helped to lay the stones and fetch clay and to chink the cracks. It was clear that she and Hoover were pals; that they were on terms of intimacy and understanding that had been denied some of his closest associates in larger affairs.

The story interested me, and I was delighted to be invited to come to a picnic one hot summer morning and assist at the completion of the dam. We drove out the Conduit Road toward Cabin John Bridge, turned off into a dirt road into the woods, and left the car. A little way through the underbrush brought us to what is known in Virginia as a "run," in New England as a "crick," and down in my part of the world as a large "branch" or small creek. In brief, a stream of the minor sort, making its way down from the hills, over a rocky bottom, to the Potomac.

The job that morning was to fetch stones, to dig clay, to make sluiceways and spills, and to put in place two overshot waterwheels. I saw Hoover walk into the water "with all his clothes on." I saw him muddy and wet to the waist, entirely absorbed and centered in what he was doing. I discovered that he could play with children on terms of absolute ease, intimacy, and equality. He wasn't at all consciously "amusing the children." He was having a good time; just as much fun as they were. It interested me that his idea of a day's holiday was to devote it to children — and to building something. It interested me even more that children accepted him on easy, equal terms. Plenty of grown people want to play with children, but don't know how. They try, but the children stand aloof. It is this quality in Hoover that I think I have discerned plus what he has done in Europe that led me to call him "The Friend of All Children." If my observation has any truth and validity, it throws a light on the passionate zeal he has shown in feeding the children of Europe since the war.

Vernon Kellogg says that, when he went to Poland in 1919 to find out the exact condition and the actual food needs of the people there, a single unpremeditated sentence in his report seemed most to catch Hoover's eye and hold his attention. It did more; it wetted his eyes. This sentence was: "We see very few children playing in the streets of Warsaw." The children were not strong enough to play. They could not run; many could not walk; some could not even stand up. It led to a special concentration of effort on behalf of the children. All this was after the armistice; after Belgium and occupied France had been fed while the war was on.

And these children of Poland were not the only ones. The Hoover family in Eastern Europe numbered at least two and a half million hungry children. I know of my own knowledge that Hoover never sought any applause for this performance. He never put himself in the way of being lionized. There is ample evidence that when he went into Belgium during the war he tried to keep his presence unknown. He would not go if he could help it to the children's canteens.

I have two stories to tell about Hoover and the Germans. They illumine both. One of them became public after the armistice, the other is told by Mrs. Hoover. Chronologically and under the rule of *place aux dames* her story comes first.

At the time of the Boxer troubles in China, the Hoovers were beleaguered in Tientsin. In their compound they had a cow and the cow had a calf. Under the circumstances, it seemed an admirable arrangement. It meant fresh milk, and if the siege continued a long time it meant fresh meat. One day the cow disappeared; stolen, of course. Hoover wanted his cow. Problem: How to find a cow in Tientsin? The town was in a state of siege. It was full of Allied troops. What to do? A happy thought. That night Hoover took a lantern, a Chinese boy, and his little calf with a halter about its neck and walked the dark streets. As they went, the calf bleated for its lost mamma. As they went through the black town in the middle of the night, there was no sound but this S.O.S. from the calf to its lost parent. Presently there came from the compound of the German troops in the town a long answering moo. Hoover advanced upon the sentry at the gate and said:

"I want my cow."

The sentry said : " Is the calf outside the calf of the cow inside ? "

Who could doubt it ?

Very well, then. The calf outside must of a necessity join the cow inside. It did. Hoover went home with his lantern, and his Chinese boy, but without his calf.

Two of the Germans who made most difficulty for Hoover and the Belgium Relief Commission were Baron von de Lancken and his assistant, Dr. Rieth. They did as much or more than anybody to make life and work difficult for the Hoover men in Belgium. Yet it was this pair that proposed to Hoover, after the armistice, to arrange with him for getting food into Germany through the Relief Commission. They received this reply by telegraph :

"Mr. Hoover's personal compliments and request to go to hell. If Mr. Hoover has to deal with Germany for the Allies, it will at least not be with such a precious pair of scoundrels."

The Belgians were often puzzled and hurt by Hoover's plain avoidance of their deep expressions of gratitude. The Belgian Government tried to thank him, but he would accept no decorations. But King Albert found a way. One day at La Panne, just after the fighting ended, Hoover was lunching with the King and Queen. After lunch the Belgian Cabinet appeared. Before them all the King created a new order without medal, ribbon, or button, or any insignia. Hoover is the only member. He was pronounced: "Honorary Citizen and Friend of the Belgian Nation."

If I am any judge of motive, this whole job of feeding the hungry in Europe was a heart impulse and not a head impulse. It was executed as a piece of efficiency engineering in terms of calories, and sustenance units, and overhead charges, and transportation and distribution expenses, but it was conceived, I believe, in terms of quick sympathy and a heart-sickness and hurt that little children should die of starvation.

Hoover is an efficiency engineer by education. He got that in the schools. It was taught him. But primarily he is an artist, with an artist's creative imagination and sensitiveness. He has been in business all his life, except through the war period. He has dealt and lived with business men. He has more influence to-day with business men than any other man in Washington. They are more at their ease with him than with any other man in the Administration. They think of him and deal with him as one of themselves. And yet he is as unlike the average business man as any could be. He wears no slight aspect of the merchant, or trader, or manufacturer, or dealer in commodities. If you met him and didn't know who he was, you would be at a loss to place him, for he has no vocational stigmata. He has led a life of romance and adventure in all parts of the world: Colorado, Mexico, Korea, the Malay Straits Settlement, South Africa, Burma, China, Australia, Russia. That is a fair spread of country.

In the end, and after his initial experiences, Hoover became a creative artist in mining. He developed a new department in his profession. He made good mines out of bad ones; successful ones out of unsuccessful ones; solvent mining concerns out of bankrupt mining concerns. He made money and a reputation in the process. He did this in the field, not on the exchanges. He dealt with materials and men and transportation on sea and land, and housing, organization, system — not bits of paper.

All that creative energy and trained efficiency and engineering skill that went first into mining, then was switched on a day's notice to Belgian relief, and again without intermission to Food Administration and back to child-feeding in Europe, is even now going full tilt in the Government at Washington.

The Department of Commerce, which is Mr. Hoover's present single nominal and titular charge, is breaking out of bounds almost every day. It is enlarging its capacities and functions. It is being remade. It will be a different thing when Hoover gets through with it. But beyond that he shares with Mr. Hughes the responsibility of being one of Mr. Harding's chief advisers. He knows about Europe and foreign affairs and conditions. He knows about labor. He is not destitute of acquaintance with the broad subject of finance.

But he doesn't know about politics. His adventure, if it may be so called, toward the Presidency was sadly mishandled, not only by Hoover, but by all those associated with him in the enterprise. There undeniably and clearly existed a widespread and strong public sentiment for Hoover for President in 1920. It had strong newspaper support from diverse and unexpected sources. Yet nothing was made of it. It was never organized ; it was never used ; it was dissipated.

Mr. Hoover is in political office now, but not "in politics." There is a difference. I haven't the faintest notion whether he intends to go into politics, whether he intends to seek political preferment — run for office ; but if he does I want to be there or thereabouts. It will be interesting. I should like to see what happens if he applies his imagination, his creative ability, and his practical engineering efficiency to national politics as it is now organized and played among us. He has proved himself in two widely separated fields one of the most competent men of this generation. He is only forty-seven years old ; a young man to be a world figure. The interesting thing and the speculative thing about him at this juncture, in his new field as a participant in the administration of government, is, what will he do next, how far will he go ? He has made himself a springboard for a tremendous leap. Will he take it ? I, for one, intend to stick around and see what happens.

UNDERWOOD: HE SUPPLIES BALM
TO GILEAD

IT is always grateful and refreshing, and particularly so on a steaming hot and humid July afternoon, to wander into the Senate galleries and observe the Honorable Oscar Wilder Underwood, senior Senator from the sovereign State of Alabama, purveying balm to the noble army of martyrs in the windowless and shut-in chamber below. He speaks to them in words of truth and soberness. Long ago he discovered that a word fitly spoken is like apples of gold in pictures of silver. To him it was not said in vain, let your speech be always with grace, seasoned with salt. Such is his habit. He is at his best when

> Dire combustion and confused events
> New hatched to the woful time

must be confronted, smoothed over, and the wrinkles taken out. In such troubled and angry crises it is his invariable rôle and his natural inclination to,

> Speak gently! 'tis a little thing
> Dropped in the heart's deep well;
> The good, the joy, that it may bring
> Eternity shall tell.

In fine, it is Mr. Underwood's great talent to bring men to be of one mind in an house. That is why he naturally and seemingly without effort rises to the leadership of any free assemblage of men.

In the present piping summer of the blessed year

Copyright by *Harris & Ewing*

SENATOR OSCAR W. UNDERWOOD

1921, on the 5th day of July, Mr. Lodge, the majority leader in the Senate, in the sticky heat rose in his place and proposed that Congress take a recess of three weeks. Mr. Underwood, as minority leader, concurred in the proposal. I quote him a bit just to show his general style:

"Senators are no different from any other set of men. They can work effectively just so far, and then their mental capacity for work breaks down and they will not work. I am talking about the men who work, who carry the responsibility of making legislation in their own heads and on their shoulders. If with this minor legislation you drive this team through July and into August, when the time comes that the House of Representatives shall send to this body the great problem that is before us, the question of solving the finances of this country and putting them on a safe and sound basis, you will not have a Senate here to attend to business, or one that is capable of attending to business.

"I do not say that theoretically. I have tried it. I was honored once by being selected as leader of the body at the other end of the Capitol. I had the same responsibility on my shoulders, and I reached the point once where I wanted to adjourn Congress through a long, hot summer, but other influences insisted that I should not do so, and I drove that Congress through a long, hot summer, and then critical legislation came up for consideration. I could not get a quorum, and the only way I brought an effective quorum there was by having passed a resolution cutting off the pay of every Member of Congress every day that he did not answer a roll call. It was unfortunate, it was drastic, but it had to be done in order to function.

"I hope the Senator will bring this to a decisive vote on the real issue. Of course, I will not interfere, as it is his business, not mine, and I will not propose an amendment, but I would like to see him extend the time one week so as to give men who live a distance time to get home and attend to their business."

At this point, Mr. Lodge broke in to say, "That is what I was going to suggest," and he at once modified his proposal to a four-weeks recess.

Before the vote was taken Mr. Underwood had a colloquy with Mr. Norris. He began his reply with these disarming words:

"Mr. President, I love the Senator from Nebraska, not for his intellectual resources, but for his goodness of character. He loves his friends and he always wants peace and enjoyment and quietude in the world, provided the balance of the Senate goes along his way."

Always the gentle approach, you see. From the very beginning that has been his style. Always he has been like that. When he first tried to come to Congress in 1894 his election was contested. He was thrown out and his Republican opponent was seated. Pleading his case, Mr. Underwood silver-tongued the boys for the first and last time of which I can find any record in his life. The young Oscar was raised in the Virginia school of manners and was early taught to say that he had had a good time when he left the party. His silver tonguing was good standard stuff, too. He used the familiar place-the-chalice-to-your-lips gambit, and these are the words he said :

"I say to you that bold was the man who stole the sacred fire of Heaven and hid it in a hollow reed, but not less bold is he who steals the elective franchise of the people of Alabama and hides it in a hollow decision of this House. You have put the bitter cup to the lips of the people of Alabama, but I warn you to pause lest some day even-minded Justice shall place the chalice to your own lips.

"I thank you, gentlemen, for your kind attention."

You see he never forgot to be polite even to his executioners. A Sydney could do no more. He was never more characteristic.

Nowadays when he is not conciliating or smoothing the wrinkled front of some parliamentary fracas, he usually talks about pig iron and steel billets and such like things, which, as young fictionists so like to say, do not intrigue me. Nor would they you, I suspect, at this juncture, and so I pass rapidly on, merely remarking for the sake of the record that Mr. Underwood is one of the acknowledged and conceded tariff experts. He knows all about the schedules from aardvarks, skins of, undressed, in bales, or alive and on the hoof, through alcohol and alum to "articles not otherwise enumerated" in the omnibus section, and paying a duty of five per cent ad valorem.

He is the author of the tariff act under which we are now protected from the pauper labor of Europe. It is supposed to be a tariff for revenue only. Mr. Underwood believes in that sort of tariff even if he does come from a strongly protectionist section of Alabama. He comes from the Birmingham district where they produce coal, iron, steel, and kindred products notably susceptible to chills and blights in the draught of foreign competition. Ask any steel master and he will tell you how steel billets stir uneasily in their sleep and are unhappy unless they are lying snug behind high tariff walls.

But all that is aside from Mr. Underwood. He is normal. Normal pulse, normal temperature, normal respiration; everything normal. He is conservative, too, but no more so than the Tropic of Cancer. He is indigenous to the north temperate zone with a mild, equable temperament, and if there is such a thing as a salubrious disposition, his is. He is quiet, bland, suave, smiling, patient, methodical, never frets, never worries; at least, he never lets you catch him doing it. Sagacious, fair-minded, steadfast, and firm in his dealings, open and aboveboard in negotiation, he has shown fine qualities of leadership in a parliamentary body.

For a great many years, I am told, there has been a saying in Alabama that no man ever became acquainted with Oscar Underwood without wanting to do something for him. No man in politics or in public life could ask for a greater asset. It comes near telling the whole story of Underwood's successful and pleasant career in politics. He has never engaged in unseemly wrangles and squabbles. He has never had to be aggressive and disagreeable to attain a goal. He has come on to be a figure in the world through the exercise of an invariable and unfailing courtesy. That is something to have done in an occupation so given to disputes, quarrels, and controversy as present-day politics. In his own party and in his own way he is as great an emollient as Mr. Harding himself. They are both healing and soothing, and give out an impression of kindliness and good-will. Mr. Underwood has found his true vocation in being leader of a Democratic minority. It is a much more difficult task than leading a majority in either branch of Congress, and, I venture to assert, there has never been a man in Washington better fitted for the job.

Although I know from bitter experience that political prophecy is the most gratuitous form of folly, I dare commit myself to the flat statement that so long as he remains in national politics Oscar Underwood will be a presidential possibility. He is, as the saying goes, presidential timber. As it seems to be our custom to elect alternately a peppery, lively President and then a sedate, calm and placid one, probably Mr. Underwood won't have a chance until 1928. But it seems a safe bet that he will be voted for again in a Democratic National Convention.

At this point, and without further delay, I must have a special paragraph devoted to the Underwood hair. No sketch of him is complete without it. It is always done, even by the apprentice biographers not yet in the union. One might as well write of Mr. Roosevelt and say nothing of his teeth, or Mr. Hughes and leave out the whiskers, or Mr. Taft and not mention his girth and his judicial temperament. It simply can't be done.

Very well, then. Mr. Underwood's hair is sleek and slick and always parted very precisely. It is never ruffled, never tousled. There is a line for every hair and every hair is on its line. Nothing but his shaving mirror ever saw a hair of his head out of place. No matter how hot it is or how cold or how the stormy winds may blow, the barometric pressure on the Underwood hair never varies. It is commonly supposed by the less observant that Mr. Underwood parts his hair in the middle. This is not accurate. I have looked down on the top of his head for fifteen years from the galleries of the House and Senate, and I ought to know. He does not part his hair on the 90th meridian or Greenwich mean time, but a little to one side ; say, daylight saving time. Then he slicks it straight down and it stays put. So much for that.

Mr. Underwood has never made the welkin ring. He is not noisy. With the arms hanging naturally by the

side and breathing from the diaphragm, he enunciates
pleasantly, slowly, distinctly. He does not orate, yet
he is an effective albeit a rather monotonous speaker.
How he escapes being unctuous is a mystery, but he
is not. His chief political and personal qualities are
patience and an even serene good temper. He displayed both of them to a notable degree one day when
he brought a wool bill into the House. It was a highly
controversial proposal and Mr. Underwood was ques-
tioned about it. Four times he was asked to explain it,
and four times he responded in detail. The fourth
questioner who had come into the chamber late was
hooted by the House when he asked to be told all about
it, but Mr. Underwood insisted on giving him the full
explanation that he had given the others and in just as
much detail. As an exhibition of courtesy and un-
ruffled good temper it won the House.

I venture to say Underwood hasn't an enemy in
either chamber. Bryan is the only politician that he
doesn't get on with and they have had some conspicuous rows, one in particular, in which Mr. Underwood
had the support and sympathy of his colleagues in
Congress.

Underwood is as typical of the New South, the business, industrial, and commercial South as dear old
Senator Morgan and General Pettus, his famous predecessors in the Senate from Alabama, were typical of
the Old South. He is unlike the run of Southern representatives in Congress even now. Also he is the only

representative from the far South who has been seriously considered and voted for in national convention
by his party for the presidency. In the Baltimore
Convention of 1912 that nominated Wilson, Underwood ran third in the prolonged balloting, and there
are not lacking politicians who believe that had his
name not been withdrawn he might have been nominated. I don't know about that. It was a tenuous
chance, if it existed at all.

Mr. Underwood has been in Congress now continuously since 1896. After the Republicans put the bitter
cup to his lips in 1894 he went home and had another
and successful try at the ensuing election. He stayed
in the House until 1915, a matter of nineteen years,
when he moved over to the Senate. It took him seventeen years to reach the leadership of the House, but for
fifteen years of that period the Democrats were in the
minority and the House leader was a Republican. He
has come quickly to be the Democratic leader in the
Senate.

Men who stay long enough in the House find their
level. Not a few men who come to Congress are leader-
less sheep. This is not a slur on Congress. It is equally
true of the arts, the professions, business and religion.
This type in the House were looking for guidance.
There came to be a saying in the ruck of the House:
"It's safe to follow Underwood." It was, too. He had
a following before the leadership came to him. The
Democrats in the House have always been kittle

cattle, inclined to stampede, not susceptible to discipline, full of views, never the ordered phalanx the Republicans have presented. Being Democratic leader was never a sinecure, but Underwood was successful. He proved himself a master hand at composing differences among his followers. By the time he came to the Senate his capacities were known. He had served his apprenticeship. The leadership passed naturally to him.

There are two sentences, says Plutarch, inscribed upon the Delphic oracle, hugely accommodated to the uses of man's life: "Know thyself," and, "Nothing too much," and upon these all other precepts depend. "Always," says George M. Cohan, "Always leave 'em happy when you say good-bye." And upon these three precepts is founded the successful career of Oscar W. Underwood who supplies the balm to Gilead.

BORAH: THE HEART BOWED DOWN

I DON'T quite know why William Edgar Borah is not a larger figure in the world than he is to-day. He has been in the Senate since 1907, a participant in the national scene with an assured place on the best platform that the country offers to any man who desires to become known and to be heard. In the Senate he has been on the successful and popular side of public issues and controversies more often than on the losing side. Yet, I suspect that he is less known than any of the outstanding figures in the whole Washington gallery.

The person who best knows Borah has been heard to say: "William would enjoy life so much better if it wasn't for all the pleasant things in the world." The secret of Borah's failure to be a popular hero despite all his admirable qualities may lie in this cryptic remark. It was made just after Borah, by the introduction of a resolution in the Senate, had reduced the Harding inauguration ceremonies from the elaborate festivities that had been planned — parade, inaugural ball, dancing in the streets, and all that sort of thing — to the simple and bald affair that it became on the East porch of the Capitol. Whatever the reason, there is a general sort of feeling current among the few that Borah has never received quite the full measure of popular applause and recognition that he has deserved. This feeling is, in part, based upon the circumstance that

SENATOR WILLIAM E. BORAH

so many other men who have done less seem somehow
to cast larger shadows.

Mr. Borah is not, as we put it in our vivid, nervous,
native tongue, a crab. Nor is he a gloom, though he
can at times approach perilously near the border line of
that category. But certainly his is the heart bowed
down. He is more inclined to view with alarm than to
point with pride.

Life to him is real, life is earnest, and there is much
to be done before the grim reaper cometh. He is a serious man full of serious thoughts and if he has a light
and festive or frolicsome side it has never been publicly
disclosed.

He is keenly sensitive, I believe, and easily hurt. My
own notion is that this quick susceptibility to adverse
criticism has kept him from thrusting himself forward
and maintaining against attack the position to which
his qualities and capacities entitle him. He has not got
a thick hide ; he feels the slings and darts of outraged
fortune. Other men less alive to possible hurt and
wounds press ahead of him.

Mr. Borah marches along in the front ranks of his
party, but he never throws himself out far in advance
of the main body of his associates. A conspicuous
instance of this trait of his character was exhibited in
1912. In that year, as all men know, Roosevelt split
the Republican Party and defeated Taft. Until the
time of the actual break Mr. Borah was allied in sympathy and, indeed, in fact with the Roosevelt faction.

He marched up to the field of Armageddon with them, but when they decided to go over Niagara Falls in the barrel that George Perkins had provided, Mr. Borah bade them a civil good-bye and *bon voyage* and returned to the Republican Party which he had really never left. He was a progressive but not a Progressive.

I don't mean in the least to imply that he was a quitter, or that he played the part of a faint-heart or traitor in that diverting episode. The whole maneuver was sharply and clearly divided into two parts. It began as a division in the Republican Party and retained that aspect until Taft was nominated. That was the first phase. Then came the matter of deciding whether or not to emulate the old monk of Siberia whose life grew drearier and drearier, and follow T. R. over the brink. Of those who went over all of them went through the whirlpool and the rapids, some of them swam ashore and made their way painfully back to their party, the others have never been heard from since.

Mr. Borah met those who came back and helped dress their wounds. He had been one with them in spirit until they made their free-will offering by jumping. As the events proved, they had made a futile gesture and Mr. Borah had shown wisdom and saved himself a circuitous journey out of his party and in again.

I recall the whole adventure because it is more illustrative and illuminative than any other incident that I know anything about in Mr. Borah's public career.

Passion and party feeling were excited and inflamed at the time. The men who had been with Roosevelt and who had to make a choice were under a stress and strain. They each acted as the general excitement affected them. They had a free choice. Now you can either say of Borah that he was faint-hearted and lacked boldness and daring or that he kept his head. For myself I choose the second alternative.

I know that he has courage, for he has proved it on other occasions, and for that matter he proved it again when he did not become a Progressive. All the pressure on him was from that side.

It was his course at that time that has left confusion in many minds about his status as between the Right and the Left. To-day in Washington you will hear him called both a conservative and a progressive. He seems to reside indeterminately in the political spectrum between the red and the violet rays. Sometimes he moves over to the left as far as the orange and again to the right as far as the indigo, but never reaches either of the two extremes.

I think it is this unconscious preference for the pastel shades instead of the raw primary colors that has, also in degree, affected wider public recognition of Mr. Borah's capacities. Where there are so many things to engage public attention and so much organized clamor, only the brightest or noisiest catch the eye and ear.

Mr. Borah has so conducted his share in public

affairs that he has never attached his name or fame to any of the admirable proposals that he has borne such a large part in making into law. I cite, by way of proof, the act for the direct election of Senators. That was a long, hard fight. Borah pressed it with resolution, with courage, with ingenuity and skill against a subtle and strong and entrenched opposition until success came. That was an excellent public service well performed, yet I venture that few now know or remember the part Borah played.

As another instance, the income tax law will serve. That is one of the fairest of all taxes in principle. It is levied directly and if the schedules or brackets are properly designed it falls equitably on all who pay it. Mr. Borah bore a part in urging the legislation through the Senate. In the debate which he carried through with skill and learning he had opposed to him some of the best minds in the Senate. That, too, I suspect is a popularly unknown part of his record.

A present modern instance is an even more striking example of how he wins races and others get the prizes. Mr. Borah introduced a resolution as an amendment to the naval bill, suggesting or inviting the President to call a conference of representatives of the United States, Great Britain, and Japan to consider the limitation and reduction of naval armaments. It hung fire for a long time. In several preliminary stages it was defeated. The opposition in the Senate was strong. Soon after President Harding came to the White

House definite word was spread abroad and brought to
the Senate that he did not wish Mr. Borah's proposal
to pass Congress. He did not wish to have his hand
forced. He was, in Frank Tinney's phrase, a architect
and he had other plans.

Borah hung on ; he pressed; he had a sound proposal.
Public sentiment grew stronger and stronger in favor of
it until one fine morning the entire opposition crumpled,
dissipated, disappeared without a sight or sound. Invi-
tations were issued not only to Great Britain and
Japan, but to France, Italy, and China, to meet in
conference at Washington to consider limitation of
armaments and other cognate matters.

Senator Johnson said of it all on the floor of the
Senate: "It was the greatest personal triumph that
has been won by a Senator in my time in this chamber."
And so it was; and for that matter, in the time of
others who have been much longer in Washington than
the bold Californian.

But Borah, oh ! where was he ? Lost in the mists.
Spurlos versenkt. Posted missing at Lloyd's. Gone
down with all hands. Effaced. As the poet so tersely
said of Lord Ullin and his daughter, "The waters
wild went o'er his child, and he was left lamenting."
They didn't even leave him a lock of hair as a keep-
sake. Overnight it became the Harding plan, the
Harding conference, the Harding disarmament policy,
and as I indite this requiem at River House on the
austere coast of Maine, it even appears that he will not

sit with other Senators who will represent the United States at the meeting which Borah and Borah alone in the Senate brought into existence. They took the cake and credit, too. It isn't fair. In a little while many will forget, and others will never know that Borah ever had any part or connection with the plan. It is another one of the large number of things that something ought to be done about.

But Mr. Borah has not been without his share of luck. He had two narrow squeaks and escaped unscathed. The first one was when he was "mentioned" for Vice-President on the ticket with Mr. Taft. There was considerable talk about this at one time, but nothing came of it. That, as it proved, was a piece of good luck. The second threat came later when it appeared for a time that Mr. Borah would be Colonel George Harvey's personally selected candidate for the Republican nomination for the presidency in 1916. He seemed to be about to take Mr. Borah up. He circled above his prospective quarry in wide swoops, emitting strange cries, and indicated the Idaho Senator by name. It didn't last long, however, but it was a puzzling performance while it did last.

All of these things, you will observe, while they have affected Mr. Borah's fame, have not checked or impaired or halted his career. While he has been attached to conspicuous proposals and conspicuous movements, they have not made him as conspicuous as lesser men have become with less cause. Such of the fruits of victory as are included under the category of fame, notoriety, publicity, a widespread recognition of work well done, have not been his. While he has missed great public fame he has achieved a reputation. He has never been "placed," but that is because he has never placed himself.

In Washington, where he has come to be a distinct figure and where he is under closer observation than he receives from the country at large, he is described by a number of adjectives. Solid is one of them, conservative another, independent a third ; to many others he is primarily a progressive, and every one agrees that he is quiet, patient, able, and of a serene temper. He is in the first flight among the Senators and always will be, whatever the quality of the membership in that chamber.

He has not in him the making of a great popular leader, because he lacks a certain daring, a certain imaginative quality that inhibits him in time of crisis from taking his political life in his hands and jumping off into the void with his eyes open. He always keeps one foot on the ground. He is not the man to head a forlorn hope, but neither is he a man to be trifled with. He makes no bones about opposing President Harding whenever he sees fit, and that is something that few care to do in these early days of the administration.

In sum : An effective, useful, intelligent public serv-ant. The people who are disappointed in him are those who expect more of him than he has in him, and I confess he gives out constantly to many the impression of having in him the motive power for longer and higher flights than he has yet essayed. Though he is fifty-six years old, and has been in the Senate fourteen years, he still creates an attitude of expectation among those who have been his close observers. They still seem to think of him as a man whose future is before him ; as a public man whose big things, whose peak achievements, are yet to be accomplished.

Be that as it may, as the policeman in O. Henry's story said, but it is this feeling of expectation he succeeds in creating that makes him the interesting and uncertain figure that he is.

LA FOLLETTE: BOB THE BATTLER

MR. LA FOLLETTE missed the train. It is only in the rarest instances that time, tide, circumstances, the hour and the man keep an appointed tryst with Destiny. One or more of them is always late. Affairs are badly ordered on this terrestrial sphere. Mr. La Follette's are a case in point. I am thinking how different things might have been with him if, in his plastic youth, or even fifteen years ago when first he came to Washington as a Senator, he had come in contact with George Santayana and read him attentively and understandingly. Particularly if he could have read Mr. Santayana's paper on English Liberty in America, which had not been written at that time. He could have learned things about us that he has never discerned or divined that would have been helpful to him in the career he laid out for himself, and which he has truncated without exactly knowing how he did it.

For Mr. La Follette and his partisans in particular, and for the general enlightenment and in the public interest, I propose here and now to do Mr. Santayana the injustice of isolating some snippets from his penetrating analysis. First he says that the thing in us that makes us what we are is the spirit of free coöperation, and that the root of it is free individuality.

"That most parliamentary measures should be

trivial or technical and really devised and debated only in government offices, and that government in America should so long have been carried on in the shade, by persons of no name or dignity, is no anomaly. On the contrary, like the good fortune of those who never hear of the police, it is a sign that coöperative liberty is working well and rendering overt government unnecessary."

"It makes impossible the sort of liberty for which the Spartans died at Thermopylæ, or the Christian martyrs in the arena, or the Protestant reformers at the stake ; for these people all died because they would not coöperate, because they were not plastic and would never consent to live the life dear or at least customary to other men. They insisted on being utterly different and independent and inflexible in their chosen systems...."

"Liberty for all pensive or rabid apostles of liberty, meant liberty for themselves to be just so, and to remain just so forever, together with the most vehement defiance of anybody who might ask them, for the sake of harmony, to be a little different. They summoned every man to become free in exactly their own fashion, or have his head cut off."

"To coöperate with anybody seems to these *esprits forts* contamination, so sensitive are they to any deviation from the true north which their compass might suffer through the neighborhood of any human magnet."

SENATOR ROBERT M. LA FOLLETTE

All this is but to say that Mr. La Follette is lacking in a certain sweet reasonableness; that he has no facility for mutual easements and accommodations; that he rubs the fur on the national hide the wrong way. When he came to the Senate in 1905 he seemed at the threshold of his larger career. His work in Wisconsin had made him a national figure. I remember there was considerable trepidation in what are euphemistically known as the highest quarters as Mr. La Follette began his progress toward Washington. There was a fear that he might take the center of the stage; that he might overshadow and, perhaps, even displace other then dominant figures in the national scene. It proved to be a baseless apprehension. The step forward was the beginning of the eclipse.

If Mr. La Follette had had a sense of proportion, discrimination, detachment of view, and even a tithe of Santayana's close and keen understanding of the national genius, there might have been another story to tell of him. He tried to hustle us into salvation, not subject to amendment or compromise. It just couldn't be done. Mr. La Follette could no more accommodate himself to becoming one of a board of directors in a joint stock limited liability company than could Peter the Hermit.

And yet if I had to make a list of the foremost public men of this generation, of men who have done constructive work in the public interest and for the public good, I should put Mr. La Follette's name well up on

the roster. I should do it unhesitatingly. Anybody
would. His work in Wisconsin alone would entitle
him to such a place.

He found the State in the hands of a sordid group of
political reactionaries, "highbinders," as they used to
be called, entrenched at home, entrenched at Washington, powerful in national politics, and devoted his
life to the restoration of the State to democracy, to
political cleanliness. He did it. His State programme
was one worthy of a great and able man. It was effective. It was intelligent. It was comprehensive. It was
thorough and constructive. He had good men en-
listed with him, men of backbone and force and imagination, men who were not afraid. He brought into the
service of the State a group of trained economists.
He made the State University the thinking machine
of the State in his reforms.

In no other State government that I know about
have such men as La Follette found been brought into
public service. It was indeed a new crowd. It was
largely made up of men never in politics, and who under
other circumstances would never have been thought
of for political office. They were precisely and literally
and actually public servants. And mighty good ones
they proved to be, too. But they never got into politics.
The men I have in mind were admirable public servants, but they never became La Follette's political
lieutenants. Frailer men got those jobs.

There is no political career in the United States that

will stand closer and more critical and searching appraisal than this State work of Mr. La Follette's. That work was done between 1880 and 1905. He was about twenty-six or twenty-seven years old when he began it. He was at the top of his stride when he came to Washington. In this summary I do not take into account the three terms that he spent in the House of Representatives before his three terms as Governor of Wisconsin. That was an interlude, or, perhaps more precisely, a prelude.

In the national field Mr. La Follette has not been successful. He has not won a following. He is to-day in the Senate an isolated figure. At one time a potential and possible candidate for the presidency, he has not to-day a vestige of a chance for that great prize. There is no faint promise that his name will ever be considered again. His self-thwarting is one of the tragedies of politics. To overturn a great evil oligarchy in Wisconsin was a work of immense difficulty. It tried his capacities and his nervous system to their utmost. The national field was too much for him. He failed because of several things. A part of the trouble lay in the inherent enormousness of the job. A part of it lay in his inability to understand the spirit of free coöperation among us that I have already invoked the aid of Mr. Santayana to indicate. A part of it lay in his personality.

He has the fatal defect in a reformer of making virtue odious, or, at any rate, tiresome and a bore.

But he is a single-minded, first-class fighter. He is no carpet knight. No matter how dark the prospects, or how dubious the outcome, he goes in and fights. Defeat does not daunt him. He does not compromise for success. One of his weaknesses lies in the fact that he will not compromise when he could do so without sacrifice of principle. He has an intrepidity of spirit which is unequaled in any man in public life I have ever known. Like Ruggles's friend, Cousin Egbert, he would fight a rattlesnake, but he would never give the snake the first two bites. This intrepidity never deserts him. It is as much to the fore in a sound course as in an unsound one.

I can very well believe what I have been told by men who have been his close associates, that there is no more charming and agreeable personality than La Follette when one is working with him and accepting his leadership not only in action, but in thought. If Mr. La Follette should chance to see this sentence, I believe he will accuse me of doing him a rank and bitter injustice, but I think that in his relations with his co-workers he always distrusts any one over whom he cannot mentally tyrannize. That has always caused him trouble. I do not know that he is wholly to blame, yet at bottom it is his fault, after all.

He has been "betrayed" or "deserted" (one somehow seems to fall naturally to these lurid terms in saying anything about Mr. La Follette) more than once by his lieutenants. The interests opposed to him

made a practice of tempting away from him one aide
after another. This enlarged and inflamed Mr. La
Follette's capacity for suspicion, made him quick to
distrust, slow to give his confidence. He has had some
bitter experiences. He takes things hard, anyhow.
These "betrayals" have made him mordant. The
very look out of his eye is one of suspicion. You are
acutely aware that he is on his guard, wary, determined not to be trapped or caught unawares. His
defenses are always up. This is an unhappy state of
mind to have to sustain. It does not make for ease or
breadth or contentment or a clear, unhampered outlook on the affairs about one.

Mr. La Follette has not been without fault in bringing about these conditions. It was difficult or impossible for really strong and able men, forceful personalities who could stand on their own feet, to subordinate
themselves as completely as they had to do while
working in close association with the Wisconsin leader.
This forced him to elevate to places of trust in his
organization one weak man after another, and they
were induced by one means and another to leave him
in the lurch. That he should have weak men about
him and that they should fail him is La Follette's one
great weakness as a political leader. After all it was
the La Follette programme they were seduced from,
not theirs. La Follette does not permit the men closely
about him to have programmes of their own, nor does
he permit them to have a sense of ownership as a joint

and common proprietor in his programme. He could not.

Persons who have been temporarily in Mr. La Follette's confidence I know have heard him speak of some of the most sincere men in public life as false to the people. He genuinely believed what he said. It was because they did not agree wholly with him in some matter of public concern then uppermost for discussion and settlement. This intolerance of spirit and quickness to suspect lost him one good collaborator after another. It is one of the reasons for his lack of success in the national field. We are an essentially kindly, tolerant people and for the most part work out our problems by rule of thumb. The general instinct is "to pull through somehow by mutual adaptation, and by seizing on the readiest practical measures and working compromises. Each man joins in and gives a helping hand, without a preconceived hand or a prior motive. Even the leader, when he is a natural leader and not a professional, has nothing up his sleeve to force on the rest, in their obvious good-will and mental blankness." (That, you will perceive, is Mr. Santayana again.) That is what Mr. La Follette does not understand. In his spirit he is a hermit, and — dare I say it with any hope of being understood by the purists — a crab.

I do not know what his fundamental political views are. To my knowledge he has never announced anything but political programmes which he hoped to have comprehended in the platforms of the Republican Party.

I do not think the fault lies in him or his work that the forces he fought in Wisconsin gained control of the State when he came to Washington. There had to be, we being what we are, a descent from the exaltation he had largely produced. But it is due and directly chargeable to his tyrannical and suspicious nature, that when he went away from Wisconsin there was no one left behind to keep the fight going successfully. Yet the whole gain was not lost. Some of the good work held. La Follette has elevated the basis on which political action must take place in Wisconsin. It bids fair to last long after his time.

And this is to be said with emphasis : La Follette is absolutely and entirely unselfish so far as seeking to reap personal profit from his public service is concerned. He is not in public office for private pelf. He is even fanatically on the level. And finally he is a man of the most prodigious industry. Every night his light is going until a late hour. He is constant in his attendance at the Capitol. He does not participate largely or frequently in the running discussion of the routine legislative grist in the Senate. He specializes in subjects that interest him and then makes a long speech that may run over two or three, or, perhaps, even four days' sessions of the Senate. He has just made such a speech this summer (1921) on British influence in or on the Shipping Board. It showed an immense amount of tedious labor. It was all illustrated with diagrams and charts such as he usually employs, but to what end? It didn't create a ripple. If it was reported in the newspapers, I didn't see it.

What Mr. La Follette says does not command wide popular attention. That is his sorry misfortune. Once he did command attention; he had that power. He has lost it. So that his present estate is doubly his sorry misfortune. He is a sincere man, an honest man, a man who seeks fervently to do the right thing, but he pitches his note too high. It is shrill. A little more kindliness, a little more tolerance, and then again a little more kindliness would have served him well. It's a pity, for he might have been a great force for good if he had had more understanding. Now he seems condemned to spend the rest of his days with the eleven obstinate jurymen. It's too bad.

LEWIS: LILAC AND LILACS

Being impressions and reflections upon observing James Hamilton Lewis, one time a Senator from Illinois, in transit to the Capitol in an F Street car at Washington

A LAVENDER shirt, a white-satin tie, and a jade stickpin; washable white chamois gloves; whiskers daintily combed, and hair that needed both brushing and cutting about the ears; a silk hat; a mottled-red cane with a silver crook; large, crusted-gold cuff-buttons shaped like dumb-bells; soft, reversed cuffs pulled well down over the hands; fawn-colored spats; light black-and-white-checked overcoat, with a blue-bordered handkerchief showing from an outside breast-pocket; a broad, black eyeglass cord falling negligently across the shirt-front; the fixed and "dressy" posture of a Leyendecker figure in a collar advertisement; an acute consciousness of self and of the interest and furtive stares of the other passengers in the car

SIMS: A FIRST-CLASS SAILOR MAN

I THINK I have never known any man who walks about the world so gayly and so unafraid as Rear Admiral William Sowden Sims. It seems incredible that he used to wear side whiskers; funny little chinchilla mudguards shaped like the breakfast rolls that the French call *brioches*. They ran down in front of his ears in the cleft between the under side of his jawbone and his neck and were closely trimmed as a privet hedge.

They were a lapse of his youth, of the period in the late seventies, of the time of Rutherford B. Hayes, when hair and the human face were in the last phase of their great battle to determine which should survive. When the armistice came and the face emerged triumphant, Admiral Sims abandoned his fancy hedge and adopted the standardized regulation: Beards, naval officers for the use of, Mark One. He has stood fast by it, and made it the regulation issue.

This partiality for whiskers is an inherited trait. The Admiral's father wore "Admiral Walkers," a long, flowing, luxuriant growth of wild and tangled clematis on either side of a clean-shaven chin. One can only say it was the fashion in those days, not a blot on the 'scutcheon, and pass quickly on to other and present aspects of our foremost naval man.

For that, of course, is precisely what he is, the first figure in the navy, the ablest officer of our generation

REAR-ADMIRAL WILLIAM S. SIMS

in the sea establishment. If there is a more competent officer on the active list of the navy, he has not made himself known and his influence felt. And I think he has come to his present estate by being unafraid.

Fear, as everybody ought to know, is the greatest deterrent to action, to enterprise, to accomplishment. It inhibits. It makes commonplace men. It reduces to a dull level. It makes for stagnation. It is a force for evil. Fearful men, timorous men run in the ruck. They may have good qualities, but they aren't the men who shove things along.

I do not seek to decry or reflect upon either the conduct or the traditions and the spirit of the army and the navy when I say that prolonged service in either branch tends to make officers, I do not say fearful and timorous, but circumspect — very, very careful and circumspect. Not in action, mind you, not toward any foe or enemy they might be sent against, but toward their superiors in their own service, toward rank, toward and about the evils of red tape and petty regulations in which they are enmeshed.

It is a situation and a condition that breeds the habit of avoidance of responsibility. It makes the game of "passing the buck" what it has become. The man who can most adroitly "pass the buck" is the man with the cleanest record. It means avoiding the hard places in the road. It means safety first to the nth power: a good rule of the road, but not necessarily a good rule of life. The man who keeps both feet on the ground and never takes a chance may be a good insurance risk, but he does not get much travel, speed, or action.

Now Admiral Sims, so far as my knowledge of him goes, has never been one of the buck-passers. When he has come under my observation, he has always been ranging like an outfielder with his head up and ready to cry, "I got it, I got it," when any one threatened to get in his way. The "buck," the responsibility, is what he has sought.

Like some of Admiral Sims's close associates in the navy, I do not take much stock in his so-called "indiscretions." To me they have always seemed more like maturely deliberated utterances. I do not think he goes off at half-cock. He knows very well what he is doing. He exercises when he sees fit, and thinks a need exists, his quality of being unafraid. He has grown in his own stature and in public esteem through these "indiscretions." Another thing he has that makes for confidence and poise and a quick willingness to back his own play, and that is, perfect health. To-day at sixty-three he is a better man physically than the average man of forty-five. He functions easily. He keeps in the pink. That perfect good health would make him chipper and gay, even without his eager, dancing spirit.

Once upon a time, now in the long ago, I went to an East Side ball in New York. Word had come to my newspaper office that there might be trouble there. It turned out to be a decorous and sedate party until a lad took his little flat derby hat, shaped precisely like the half of a Rocky Ford melon, and shied it out into the middle of the floor. "Hooray for hell," he said. Then it began. I think Admiral Sims has a little something of that spirit in him. There is a certain gayety and joyousness of spirit about him that likes a shindy. It is a quality the Irish have. It made Donnybrook Fair famous. Admiral Sims has enjoyed his controversies. He has carried them on in a spirit of high good humor. They have stimulated him. He is always a gay companion when he is under fire and engaged in a cut and thrust enterprise.

In sharp contrast with this carefree aspect of his personality is his methodicalness of method. He has a remarkably retentive memory, really one of these of-course-I-place-you-Mr.-Addison-Sims-of-Seattle minds. But he does not depend on this memory alone. He reënforces and documents it. His books, papers, records, maps, etc., are kept in a precisely ordered, cross-indexed filing system with a place for everything and everything in its place. One of his aides once told me :

"I recall one day in Newport when the Admiral was laid up in bed with a slight cold (I never knew him to have anything more serious than this) receiving a note from him asking me to send him a certain paper that was in his office. The memo which I received from him was a sketch of his office bookcase with all of the books on the two upper shelves indicated by name and the location of the paper he wanted indicated with reference to one of these books. I found the paper exactly where he said it was and sent it to him forthwith. That bookcase, like everything else he has ever seen, was photographed on his mind and the negative filed away for future reference."

This is not to say that Admiral Sims is a man who loves details and buries himself in them. He knows how to keep subordinates busy, and to distribute work as well as any man I have ever known. I only seek to indicate that he can be carefree and joyous when he is in a row because he has carefully and thoroughly prepared his position before he begins to fight; to support my contention that he does not go off at half-cock.

He does not play for his own hand, either, his own personal, selfish reward, aggrandizement, and preferment. He is bound up in the navy. He has been honest with himself and the country he serves so conspicuously. I frankly confess that I was not wholly and perfectly sure of his disinterestedness until the World War. In some of his other enterprises that brought him into the public eye and notice there was a possibility that a yearning for personal acclaim and a desire to lift himself to become a figure in the world might have been one of his motives. There were never lacking persons to whisper this charge.

But the great war was the searching test. Admiral Sims could have so managed his affairs and the affairs

of the navy abroad, so conducted himself toward the
Navy Department and the powers at home in Washington, could have been so smooth, so pliant, so discreet, so accommodating and complaisant, so adroit in
taking the easiest way, that he might have returned
full of honors — which he would not have deserved. I
think there is no doubt he could have so contrived his
business that he would have been made a full Admiral
for life with the thanks of Congress, and mayhap a
sword or some additional token. But he was never
tempted to advance his personal interests at the expense of the public interest or an efficient prosecution
of the war to an early and unimpeded conclusion. He
might have taken to the water and paraded himself
before a gaping continent had he so chosen, and only a
handful of people in all the world would have known
that he was play-acting. To the others he would have
been a hero.

Instead, as was his duty and obligation, he kept a
careful, orderly record of all that was done and all
that was not done that affected our participation in the
war at sea. Then when the war ended he came home
and had it out with Mr. Josephus Daniels and the
Navy Department. He submitted a piece of constructive, documented, supported, and attested criticism of
naval administration. He pressed it boldly and fear-
lessly. He forced a controversy. He got a Senate in-
vestigation and the whole naval conduct of the war
thoroughly aired and investigated. He was sustained

in his contentions and his criticisms. It was a public service. It was not the first nor the second time he had stood up against the Navy Department and won. It was the third time.

In 1901, after trying in vain over a long period through official channels to get action and remedy, Admiral Sims wrote directly to President Roosevelt over the head of the Navy Department and charged that the navy couldn't shoot for beans. He proved it by the target practice records. It was a disillusioning and disconcerting revelation. It raised a rumpus. Roosevelt brought Sims home from China and put him in charge of the navy's target practice.

"Do exactly as he says for eighteen months," said Roosevelt. "If he does not accomplish something in that time, fire him."

Sims was inspector of target practice for six and one-half years, until our naval gunners became the best shots in the world. Whether they have retained that eminence, I do not know. There was some good shooting in the North Sea a little while ago in which we did not participate. But if we are not still the best naval gunners in the world, we have not fallen back to the humiliating inefficiency that was ours prior to Sims's criticism. That was a piece of effective constructive criticism in naval gunnery.

His second notable encounter with the Navy Department grew out of his first. He brought about a radical change and improvement in naval construction.

Roosevelt helped him in this, too. From 1900 to 1907
Sims constantly poured into the Department a flood
of reports in which he repeatedly charged gross errors
of construction in our fighting ships. They weren't
properly protected, they weren't properly designed,
there was virtually nothing about them that was not
wrong; they were armored under water but not above,
the guns lay so low that in a sea they were awash;
the gun apertures in the turret were too large and
offered no protection to the gun crews, the magazines
were exposed and badly placed.

"The Kentucky is not a battleship, at all. She is the
worst crime in naval construction ever perpetrated by
the white race," was one descriptive comment.

By the beginning of 1908 these charges and asser-
tions were appearing in public print. Sims was threatened with court-martial. Secretary Metcalfe, who
didn't know or even suspect that President Roosevelt
was privy to all that was going on, wrote Sims a formidable letter. But Roosevelt quietly squelched all
that. The present design and construction of American battleships dates from those criticisms and that
issue forced by Sims.

Twice it was thought the part of "discretion" by
the President or the Navy Department to administer
Pickwickian reprimands to Admiral Sims for his "indiscretions." At the Guildhall in London in 1910 he
said: "If the time ever comes when Great Britain is
menaced by a European coalition she can count upon

every ship, every dollar, and every drop of blood of her kindred beyond the sea." Of course, this was a great "indiscretion," doubly so because of the fact that it was true. Sims was reprimanded, and then when his prophecy came true was dispatched to London to give the aid he had promised ; that he had stepped outside his jurisdiction to promise.

His latest "indiscretion" was a frank public expression of his views about a faction or an element of the Irish people. It inevitably caused a commotion and Sims was duly reprimanded by the Secretary of the Navy — and then went across the street and spent a pleasant social hour by invitation with the Commander-in-Chief of the Army and Navy, the President of the United States. The next three months he spent in endeavoring to answer all the letters, telegrams, and messages of warm commendation he received. The flood of these came to be so great that he had to have a form letter of reply printed.

Sims is a keen professional. The navy is his be all and end all. He thinks ahead. He tries to peer into the future. He has a clear professional vision and a working imagination. He has never become a "shellback" in the navy.

In the present rivalry between the surface craft and the aircraft at sea his mind is veering toward the aircraft as something new and full of undeveloped possibilities. He has been urgent before committees of Congress in asking for airplane carriers. These carriers may prove to be the capital ship of the immediate and imminent future. This eager, almost boyish, quality of his mind that makes him quick to receive new ideas, new things, is a thing that makes him likable as a companion.

Young officers in the navy are his warmest and most enthusiastic admirers. One of them told me: "There has always been a team whenever we were at sea with Admiral Sims as the captain, elected to this position by the team because he has always been the best member on it. His discipline has always been a discipline of appreciation rather than a discipline of fear."

A fine, gay, upstanding sailor man. That he is unafraid is the thing to know and remember about him.

PERSHING: BEAU SABREUR; 1921 MODEL

WE are adjured to laugh where we must, be candid where we can, but vindicate the ways of God to man. The sentiment, as, of course, you know, is Alexander Pope's. It seems to me admirable. Honesty is my policy. Frankness is my besetting sin.

So much by way of preface to my confession that I never even saw General Pershing until the day he drove from the Union Station to his hotel in Washington months after the armistice. I am one of perhaps a million of the expeditionary force who never laid eyes on General Pershing in France. In my particular case it was not his fault, but mine, that we never met. I dodged him. This was not rudeness on my part, but fear, a sentiment toward our chieftain that I found myself sharing with thousands. My own particular fear, which also was shared, was that if the great man ever came upon me I would be harshly and severely chided about the details of my uniform, and perhaps sent home for not being dressed according to regulations.

Two things I quickly discovered as I approached the zone of the armies in my new capacity as a reserve officer. One was that it was a sign of bad luck to cross the path of the General, or as he was commonly called behind his back, the Old Man. The other was that it made a lot of difference how you were dressed. These two factors of warfare as they oppressed or concerned

BEFORE　　　　　　　　　　　　　　　　　AFTER

WHAT THE WORLD WAR DID FOR ERAL PERSHING

the individual were inseparably entwined. One hinged
upon and was a part of the other. Fear of, or thought
about the foe, was a minor consideration unless and
until one immediately confronted him.

It was borne in upon one that this was not only a
siege war, and a war of position, but a war of detail.
Little things counted. At London, and before I reached
France, I learned that General Pershing signed his
communications to the War Department as, "Commander-in-Chief, American Expeditionary Force,"
and that the replies from Washington were addressed
to "Commanding General, A.E.F." This difference
in designation was much commented upon, and importance attached to it by the military minds.

The Pershing zone of influence abroad extended to
and included London. I bought a water-proof cap
cover there and within an hour a captain of coast
artillery checked me with, "That's not regulation."
I held out that it was a reasonable precaution, and I
thought allowed. It ended in a bet of half a crown and
an appeal to the book of regulations. I won, but the
captain gave in reluctantly.

"I don't believe the Old Man would stand for it. If
I were you I wouldn't wear it in France. It might get
you in wrong."

He was my friend, and I knew wished me well. The
dawning of fear came here.

The shadow of General Pershing's interest in what
the well-dressed soldier is wearing next fell upon me

when I was inducted into the harness of the Sam Browne belt. While the transport that took us across lay at the dock in New York I stood on the upper deck watching the troops pour into the ship. A young officer came aboard with his men, and fifteen minutes later started back down the gangplank of the dock. In the interval he had put on a Sam Browne belt. There came a roar from his colonel who stood near me. "Get back on the ship and take off that belt. Where do you think you are, in France?"

This hinted at rites and mysteries that were beyond my ken. Henry Ford had failed in his effort to get the boys out of the trenches by Christmas. I began to suspect that getting the boys into the trenches before the next Christmas would want a bit of doing, until we were all taught how to dress before we could fight a German.

Some day some person versed in the psychology of the trivial ought to make an exhaustive study of the attitude of the military mind toward the Sam Browne belt. I am concerned here only with General Pershing's attitude. He was for it. Officers leaving for France could not wear the belt. It was not a part of their equipment. No provision was made for supplying them. But when they touched the foreign strand they must have one. It was General Pershing's orders, and whatever else may be said of his orders, they were obeyed. He commanded and everybody knew it to the uttermost fringes of his authority.

At each of the base ports in France a supply of Sam
Browne belts was kept on hand for sale to arriving
officers. In France we were considered half naked if we
did not wear it at all times and on all occasions. Even
in the far rear of the army along the line of the S.O.S.
the disappointed lads who had been hung up in their
desire to get to the front, in their quiet and peaceful
messes at dinner wore the Sam Browne. It was General Pershing's orders.

But when we got home again we were met at the
dock in Hoboken with a large pink printed order in-
forming us in heavy black type that on no account
must we leave the transport wearing Sam Browne
belts, under penalties and provisions made and provided. Officers were stationed at the gangways as we
came ashore to see that the order was carried out and
obeyed.

But when General Pershing came home there was no
one to tell him to take his belt off and he continued to
wear it right along until he was made Chief-of-Staff of
the army. Then he didn't even hesitate. One of his
very first orders was: "On and after July 15, 1921, the
Sam Browne belt will be worn at all times by all commissioned officers outside their quarters when in
service coat, and with the O.D. shirt if under arms. . . .
The Liberty belt now obtainable from the Quartermaster Corps is an authorized form of the Sam Browne
belt."

General Pershing has done for the Sam Browne belt

what Kosciusko and George Washington and Patrick Henry did for liberty, what Lincoln did for the Union, what "Babe" Ruth has done for the home run — he has attached his name and fame to it; he has raised it to a high estate among us. It is his great war souvenir.

But in my preoccupation with this great triumph of army dress reform I have drifted away from other and lesser things that have contributed to an impression of the aspect of General Pershing's characteristics that I share with so many who served under him in France, and who never came in intimate contact with him. We had neither the desire nor the competency to appraise his military capacities and qualities. That wasn't any of our business. He was the head of the show, and what he said went, and we knew it. What we were interested in and wanted to know about were his qualities and idiosyncrasies as they affected us. We wanted to run with the grain, not against it. We learned early that he cared about the niceties of dress.

I crossed the North Atlantic Ocean bareheaded in one of the coldest Januarys in the history of the world, because of one of his orders. He had forbidden the use of campaign hats in France, and I knew it, so I didn't buy one when I started over. The first order issued on the transport was that campaign hats and campaign hats only should be worn on the voyage across. I was just whipsawed.

I was always being reminded of my clothes, indirectly and informally, but traceable back through

military channels to General Pershing. Of course, he
never knew anything about or heard of the service
coat or tunic that I got in Paris, but he had so impreg-
nated and impressed those who had been in contact
with him that he didn't have to see it to have the news
reach me as to what he would have thought about it
and said about it if he had seen it. Through some mis-
adventure or lack-wittedness on the part of the French
tailor the buttons were sewn on upside down. The
eagles with outspread wings were standing on their
heads. I thought I would never hear the end of it. For
the sake of the record I wish I had kept an actual count
of the number of times I was accosted: "Better not
let the Old Man see those buttons," or, "Say, you are
taking a big chance if the General ever lays his eyes on
you. He'll spot those buttons a mile off."

I fear I very nearly spoiled the war for one officer
whom I saw frequently and who became a closely
attached subordinate of General Pershing, for I dug
in on the button line and never did have them reversed.
But I was not foolhardy. I had been impressed. I
didn't throw myself in the way of General Pershing. I
had two narrow squeaks but got away unscathed. The
first was at Mollien-au-Bois when the Thirty-Third
Division lay there. General Pershing came up one day
to distribute some decorations. An alert M.P. warned
me of his presence and I lay below the horizon until he
left. I was not alone, either. The second time was
when I ran into Ligny and found First Army Head-

quarters and General Pershing there. I walked straight into the lion's den, all unknowing. One of the aides said, "Captain, your buttons are upside down," but I was used to that and flitted before harm could befall me.

There were other indications and signs, too, that percolated through the army of the interest in dress that was felt by the high command. They came through to us as matters which General Pershing set store by. There was a ban on cord breeches lighter in color than the khaki tunic, until it was discovered that the General had adopted this English fashion. To wear a service coat or tunic with a slit, or as the tailors call it, a vent, in the back was almost as heinous an offense as giving information to the enemy, until again General Pershing was converted to it. I think it never became regulation.

And as for the man who sought to have bellows pockets on his jacket, he had swapped his nationality for a mess of pottage. I could go on and cite other instances of this interest in the niceties of dress that so impressed me as one of General Pershing's major concerns. Take, for example, the complex case of the boot, the puttee and the leggin and their relationship to the spur. Much might be said about that, but I refrain. A japery ran about for a time: "Why do aviators wear spurs?" The answer was: "So that they will not be mistaken for cavalrymen."

Now I have to cite by way of confirmation of the

General's interests, first, the pictorial record of his sartorial rise and progress through the war. Even if he did not altogether succeed in making the body of officers of the army a daily hint from Paris to the Allies and the cruel foe, he at least succeeded in reaching new high altitude levels in his own attire. I submit that he was the best-dressed man on our side that the war produced. The change and the progress are indicated by the two portraits that precede this chapter. One of them was taken before the General went to France, the other after his enlightening experience abroad.

I now summon as a witness Brigadier-General Charles G. Dawes, Pershing's great friend and admirer, whose experience was my experience. He confirms my impression. He did not discover General Pershing's zeal for the niceties of dress by indirection and hearsay as I did, but directly and at first hand. He wrote in his diary that General Pershing's mind "is certainly open to details, no matter how impressive the surroundings," and tells this story:

"After he [Pershing] had finished his conference with General Foch, he was standing across the road from me and some Frenchmen, with General Harbord, waiting for Foch to take his automobile for his trip to Abbéville to see Haig. I saw him looking at me, notwithstanding the sound of the cannon, and the general surroundings, with the look of mingled friendliness, admonition, and concern which characterizes his expression during some of my interviews with his better-disciplined military associates. It led me to make a hasty self-appraisement of my attitude, in which, however, I could surmise no fault. He spoke to Harbord and the latter walked across the road to me. As Harbord carefully buttoned up my overcoat, which was opened, including the hooks at the top, he murmured in my ear, 'This is a hell of a job for a Chief-of-Staff — but the General told me to do it.'"

I am indebted to General Dawes for so amply confirming my impression and for setting down the incident in his book, "A Journal of the Great War." It was just the touch I needed to give me complete confidence in the validity of my own vivid impression.

By way of further confirmation, there are the orders signed John J. Pershing, General of the Armies, that began to issue from the War Department as soon as the General became Chief-of-Staff. The bestowal of the Sam Browne belt was one. Another permitted the use of tabards attached to the bugles or trumpets of company buglers. A tabard is a rectangular banner of silk or cloth hanging from the crook of a bugle or trumpet and its design follows that of the coat of arms or badge of the organization as approved for use on the organization colors or standard. The buglers at General Pershing's headquarters in France were permitted tabards. They were a novelty and decorative to a degree. Now they are regulation. Another statement from the War Department announced that the present high, stiff collar of the uniform coat would not be

abandoned in favor of the open-throat roll collar such
as the English wear. Other orders related to the wearing of white uniforms, badges, and decorations.

I have confined myself perforce to polishing and
presenting this one facet of our hero's personality
because it was the one bright impression of him that I
brought away from France with me. Of his qualities
as a strategist, a tactician, an administrator, I have
no material for judgment. Certainly in France and
since he came home he has kept his head, he has not
been indiscreet in any small particular. He has not
talked. He has not gone out of his way to seek popular
applause. He has not tried to make occasion for ova-
tions. He has spoken only when called upon to speak,
and when he has said anything he has confined himself to the business in hand. The armies in France did
not idolize or idealize him. They did not bring him
home as a great popular hero. They did not want him
as a candidate for President.

But this attitude of indifference was not confined to
General Pershing; it extended to all the other commanding generals of our forces in France. The great
bulk of the men who went over were glad enough to be
through with military ways and professional military
men when the end came. I think they gave General
Pershing full credit for everything he did in France. I
think the common feeling among them was and is
that he did his part as well as he knew how, and they
did theirs in the same fashion. Nobody was inclined
to take the matter any further. So here it rests.

TAFT: IN PORT AT LAST

At last Mr. Taft has come to his journey's end. He has been a long time on the way. Ever since I have known him, and that is since 1905, he has been the "logical candidate for the next vacancy on the Supreme Bench." Now we can hope to see his most famous possession, his judicial temperament, functioning. It has been long maturing and preparing for the test. But I want Mr. Taft to have his full due and credit.

It is now widely and commonly said that he is Chief Justice of the Supreme Court. That is inaccurate. There is no such place, post, or employment under our form of government. Mr. Taft is Chief Justice of the United States. His colleagues are Associate Justices of the Supreme Court of the United States. There are two great offices at the top of the heap as we have organized society on this continent: President of the United States and head of the executive branch; Chief Justice of the United States and head of the judicial branch. Mr. Taft is the first man in our history to have been elected to the one and appointed to the other.

His being President was an unhappy adventure. He approached it reluctantly; he never was at ease when he was in the White House, and he never got any fun or satisfaction out of the job. Only Vermont and Utah (or was it Nevada?) wanted him to have a second term.

His coming to be President at all was as odd a thing

THE CHIEF JUSTICE OF THE UNITED STATES

as ever happened within my knowledge of politics. It was known to all the world, toward the end of 1907, that Mr. Roosevelt would award the Republican nomination for the presidency in 1908. There was to be no contest about it. Mr. Roosevelt was to give it to the one he loved best. He made up his mind slowly because he wanted a winner. When he first talked with me about his problem, he had narrowed his choice down to Mr. Taft and Mr. Root. He weighed and balanced those two, one against the other. He talked with a good many people first and last who might have a slant on public opinion. Mr. Root was sent to South America to "get a reputation," as the saying is. When he got back home he went out to Kansas City and made a speech to the Knife and Fork Club. That had been arranged, too. But the Middle West didn't rise. Nobody rose. Mr. Roosevelt began to turn more toward Mr. Taft, and to complain that Mr. Root "had no sense of a public."

During those days Mr. Taft knew, of course, what was going on, and he used to tell his confidants that he would never become a candidate for the nomination; that he had no aspirations to become President; that his whole ambition and desire would be completely satisfied if he could be on the Supreme Court. He wanted that and nothing else. A place on the highest bench was the summit of every lawyer's desire, he was a lawyer and nothing else, and eager only for preferment on the judicial side. But in the end he was overborne, and capitulated as was too often the case later when urgent pressure was applied.

He did not make an eager candidate after he was nominated. He didn't like campaigning for votes. He didn't like standing up and telling the people what a wonder he was, and how they would all be prosperous and happy and have good crops and good business if they made him President. He didn't believe it himself. He didn't like any of the campaign hokum. It all bored him to extinction. He was blue and depressed about his prospects throughout the canvass.

I joined him at Cincinnati when he began his first speech-making trip. It was very hot. Mr. Taft had a special train. His first speech was to be made at George Ade's farm near Brook, Indiana.

In those days the candidate had a girth and conformation that required freshly pressed trousers every day, especially in the hot weather, so he had a Filipino valet. But some of the shrewd boys decided that Felipe should not be taken on the journey through the corn belt. The honest yeomanry of those parts might take it amiss. The little brown brother sneaked aboard the train, however, and had to be shoved off when he was discovered after an hour or so. Freed of its incriminating freight, the train went on to Brook. There followed a dusty ride out to the farm, where all the people from far and near had gathered, a fine lot of men and women, just about the best and soundest we produce.

Outdoors on a rough platform under the trees Mr.

Taft fired his opening gun of the campaign. At this late day no harm can come of saying that it was a "dud." The shell did not explode. Mr. Taft read to them from a typewritten manuscript his views on the Philippines, and an adequate coast defense system. It was something dire. The temperature went down, down, down. The Indiana politicians who were running the show were making the S.O.S. signal. They rushed up their reserves. Jim Watson was called on to save the day. He done noble. He had nothing to say and he said it grandly. He ran his fingers through his hyacinthine locks, pulled out the *vox humana* stop, and gave them the grand old dope, the grand old party, the grand old flag — the heart-warming stuff they had come to hear.

The whole performance was symbolical, was it not, in a way, of the subsequent history of the Taft Administration? He was always getting in holes and having to be pulled out. At Brook that day, the *cognoscenti* there assembled came to the conclusion, later amply verified, that Mr. Taft was no politician.

Mr. Taft was never detachedly appraised until he became President. While he was in the Philippines and in the War Department, he was in the shadow of other men. He was an agent, not a principal. Everybody liked him. He soon became known as one of the honestest men that ever stepped foot in Washington, and as lacking in all craft and guile as a child. He was too frank and naïve for his own good. He believed — oh, so simply — that there was such a thing as friendship in politics. And no obligation rests more heavily on Mr. Taft's shoulders than the obligations of friendship.

When he came to the White House there was not a more popular man in public life in the United States. He hadn't a single political enemy. Democrats vied with Republicans in expressing their good-will. It didn't last long — just through the Payne-Aldrich Tariff session and the Winona speech. After that everything seemed to go wrong. Mr. Taft couldn't please anybody. He tried so hard to please everybody.

I recall two criticisms of that period, so obviously intended to be fair and so accurately describing Mr. Taft's character and characteristics in the White House as to have stood the test of time. First: "Mr. Taft has tried to be everybody's friend, and as usual in such cases he has not succeeded in fully pleasing anybody. The public knows that he is honest and sincere and patriotic, but it is not sure that he measures up to the full requirements of his office. It would like a little more independence, a little less partisanship, a little more reliance upon his own common sense, a little more courage, a little less veneration for the elder statesmen of the Republican Party, and a little less organization politics."

And this: "The peculiar weakness of Mr. Taft as a directing force, the peculiar deficiency he has exhibited in respect of political sagacity, has never been more conspicuous than in this complacent view of his own defeat. After staking his prestige on a particular issue, after identifying himself with a legislative programme in such a way as to leave no doubt that he regarded its adoption as indispensable to the success of his administration, he seems ready to accept defeat as a thing for which he cannot justly be held in any way accountable. . . . He has shown a certain mechanicalness, a certain want of that vital touch without which a powerful hold on public affairs is impossible. . . . A large part of the influence that a President can wield, through the pressure of public opinion, comes from the fact that the nation listens to him as it listens to no one else. But the retention of this position of advantage, the continued possession of this great leverage bestowed upon him by his office, is dependent upon his husbanding of his resources. If he is ready to speak every day in the week and to point out his thoughts or feelings just as they happen to come, he will soon find his audience wanting. A want of perspective, a lack of the feeling that some things must be done and that others are best left alone, has been no small part of the cause of Mr. Taft's troubles."

I have chosen to revive here these two acute comments because they fairly represent the intelligent criticism to which Mr. Taft was subjected. He has none of the salient traits that mark out and distinguish natural leaders of men in the field of politics. He came into office on the strength of the political prestige and authority of Theodore Roosevelt, and he received a larger vote than was ever cast prior to that time for any other President of the United States.

He did the best he could. God help him, he could do no more. He went into it to oblige a friend. He had no other desire than the best interests of the United States. He was out of his element. He had no political sagacity to begin with, and he never acquired any. He could never accommodate himself to leadership, and the President must be a leader. Mr. Taft used to call himself "titular leader" of his party.

But I think the new Chief Justice will be happy in the Supreme Court. He will not have to consider politics, or expediency, or the claims of personal friendship, or be subjected to powerful and urgent pressure from any quarter. These have always proved his stumbling-block and the cause of his undoing. Heretofore through his career since 1900 he has been doing what other people wanted him to do, a draft man, first in the Philippines, then Secretary of War, then the presidency. All the time his heart and his inclination were turned toward the bench. Where the heart is there also the treasure lies. A true saying.

Now, at last, Mr. Taft has got his chance to follow on where his heart has been calling. He has come to hold the high place in the most peaceful haven that this troubled world affords. Having once reached it, the traveler lives in a serene, untroubled air. He is as immune from criticism as from punishment for his actions. He is beyond the reach of all mankind ; subject only to the laws of God and the dictates of his own conscience. There he may dwell until gathered to his fathers, for though after a certain specified period he, if he so desires, may retire on full pay, there is no mandatory requirement that he shall ever give over the work John Marshall began.

The life of a Justice on the bench of the Supreme Court of the United States, as Mr. Taft well knows, comes as near being an ideal way to spend one's allotted span of years on this sphere as is permitted in this sadly ordered world. If he be properly selected, the Justice loves his work. What he has to do affords him the chief pleasure of his days. He has the consciousness that it is important work ; that his decisions will affect for good or ill not only men now living, but, in many instances, the unborn sons of men. Inherent in a seat on the bench are great powers and grave responsibilities, which may be exercised in absolute detachment from all worldly interests and without fear, favor, or hope of reward. The Justice is far removed from daily temptation, from importunities and pleadings, from the demands and exactions of friendships, and from all the little intimate things that swerve the cold processes of reason in the forming of the average man's judgments.

The haven into which Mr. Taft has come is the only institution of our government with which long and close contact and acquaintance do not breed familiarity or an easy contempt. Persons much about the Capitol at Washington come quickly, too quickly in most instances, to view the daily life and processes of the House of Representatives and the Senate with a full and keen appreciation of their defects and weaknesses. Living here without a proper perspective, the tendency is to exaggerate the little bits of cowardice, the indirect purposes and motives, and not to see and remember that at the core both branches of the national legislature are essentially sound.

One even comes in time to view the presidency without illusions. Behind all the hurrah and the clamor is a greatly overworked human being like ourselves subject to the temptations and perils and trials that beset all of us, whether we be eighteen-dollar-a-week bookkeepers in grain and feed stores or directors of great enterprises involving millions of capital.

When Mr. Taft became Chief Justice, he discovered that he had inherited a "body servant." The office seems to be hereditary, for some of the men now serving were preceded by their fathers. They are all negroes, of course, and they know the forms and traditions of the court to the last fine point. Under the guise of serving, they rule the private life of the Justices with the iron authority and discipline that persons in the South have long been familiar with in old family servitors. Mr. Justice Woods, who was appointed to the bench by President Garfield, is reported to have said soon after he took his place on the court:

"My body-servant is the most annoying thing I
have experienced. The fellow is the first man I see in
the morning and the last man I see at night. He forces
his way into my bedroom in the morning and orders
me down to breakfast, taking my order himself to the
cook. I cannot get rid of him in any way. He haunts
me all the time. I try to think of places to send him,
but he is back again as quick as lightning. That fellow
will be the death of me."

One of the stock and prized anecdotes about the
court relates to a young lawyer who was very earnestly
pleading to establish a point before the court. While
he was still in the full course of his appeal, one of the
Justices leaned over the bench and interjected crisply :

"But that is not the law."

The young lawyer was abashed, but only for a moment before he retorted, "It was the law until the
court spoke." The sum of our attitude toward the
court has never been better exemplified.

Mr. Taft, as President, himself illustrated this attitude. In a special message on the interstate commerce
and anti-trust laws, communicated to the two Houses
of Congress on January 7, 1910, Mr. Taft said among
other things : "Now the public, and especially the
business public, are to rid themselves of the idea that
such a distinction (as between 'good trusts' and 'bad
trusts' or as between 'reasonable' restraint of trade
and 'unreasonable' restraint of trade) is practicable
or can be introduced into the statute. Certainly,

under the present anti-trust law no such distinction exists. . . ."

The Supreme Court, as is well known, took an opposing view in the Standard Oil opinion. A group of persons so large as to be called fairly a throng went to the White House on the day following the court's decision, and sought audience with President Taft. Each of them had equipped himself with a copy of the message containing this paragraph. They all wanted some comment from Mr. Taft. Let me quote the current accounts in the newspapers, which I know to be trustworthy:

"When it was called to the President's attention that in his message to Congress of January 7, 1910, he expressed doubt of the practicability of defining 'good' and 'bad' trusts, he said that whatever had been his opinions, he abandoned them when the Supreme Court spoke.

"The President would not discuss the decision at all. He directed the attention of some of his callers to the fact that, before a decision is handed down by the Supreme Court, every one is entitled to have his personal view of the matter, but that after the decision has been rendered it is the law of the land, and every law-abiding citizen is bound to bow to it."

Mr. Taft has a great respect for law, authority, and orderly processes, and I am sure he will find it grateful and refreshing to be in an atmosphere and environment where he can function in a vacuum free from pressure, free from naggings, and reach conclusions and decisions that nobody can or will question. It is the ideal condition he has long sought. If he doesn't make secure and lasting his own reputation, it will be his own fault.

THE END

𝕮𝖍𝖊 𝕽𝖎𝖛𝖊𝖗𝖘𝖎𝖉𝖊 𝕻𝖗𝖊𝖘𝖘

CAMBRIDGE . MASSACHUSETTS

U . S . A